215

THE FACE OF THE PAST

The face of the past

THE PRESERVATION OF THE MEDIEVAL INHERITANCE IN VICTORIAN ENGLAND

CHARLES DELLHEIM
Department of History
Arizona State University

CAMBRIDGE UNIVERSITY PRESS

Cambridge
London   New York   New Rochelle
Melbourne   Sydney

Published by the Press Syndicate of the University of Cambridge
The Pitt Building, Trumpington Street, Cambridge CB2 1RP
32 East 57th Street, New York, NY 10022, USA
296 Beaconsfield Parade, Middle Park, Melbourne 3206, Australia

First published 1982

Printed in the United States of America

Library of Congress Cataloging in Publication Data
Dellheim, Charles, 1952–
The face of the past.
Bibliography: p.
Includes index.
1. England – Civilization – 19th century.
2. Historic buildings – England – Conservation
and restoration.   3. Historic sites – England –
Conservation and restoration.   4. Architecture –
England.   5. England – Antiquities.   I. Title.
DA533.D43   942.081   82–4486
ISBN 0 521 23645 2   AACR2

FOR MY MOTHER AND FATHER

The brief description of the characteristic merit of the English Constitution is, that its dignified parts are very complicated and somewhat imposing, very old and rather venerable; while its efficient part, at least when in great and critical action, is decidedly simple and rather modern...Its essence is strong with the strength of modern simplicity; its exterior is august with the Gothic grandeur of a more imposing age.
— Walter Bagehot, *The English Constitution* (1867)

Contents

Illustrations

Illustrations

Preface

It is a striking paradox that as England became the first industrial nation, it became increasingly fascinated by its preindustrial
past and in particular its medieval inheritance. I began to
study the historical problem of why this occurred by examining how poets and novelists, painters and architects, historians and reformers used particular aspects of the medieval
legacy for their own purposes. But soon enough the direction
of my research changed as I recognized that the concern with
the Middle Ages was confined neither to an elite of artists and
thinkers nor to the critics of modern civilization. The experience of living in Britain for two years while working on this
book impressed upon me the importance of the physical presence of the past to the imagination. Hence, I turned my scholarly attention to general cultural activities such as local archeology
and tourism, historic restoration and preservation, and architectural historicism, because they best revealed the face of the
past experienced by Victorians. Although much of the material used in this book is therefore visual, it is intended as a
study in cultural history rather than architectural or art history. It explores how Victorians regarded, treated, and rehabilitated medieval artifacts in order to illuminate their cultural
attitudes and values rather than aesthetic styles and techniques.
The broadest aim of this book is to contribute to our understanding of the interaction between industrialism and culture
in modern Britain by examining how Victorians reworked tradition to suit the needs of their unprecedented society.

It should go without saying that the activities studied here are salient features of our own cultural landscape. The tourist in search of historic ruins and riches in the name of personal enlightenment, social status, or holiday diversion is a nearly mythological, if hardly beloved, figure. Every summer the British await with ambivalent emotions the descent of sightseers anxious to inspect historic towns, regions, and buildings. Tourism, as everyone knows, has become a lucrative industry. Many civilizations have plundered the past, but none has packaged it as skillfully as ours has done. The cause of historic preservation has also become increasingly popular in recent years for several reasons. The fine craftsmanship and elaborate ornamentation of historic buildings has become respectable, indeed fashionable, once more as the functionalist dogmas of Modernist architecture are undermined. Rehabilitating historic buildings seems all the more attractive because it is usually less expensive than building new ones. Perhaps the most striking aspect of contemporary preservation is the movement to find new uses for old fabrics, by retaining facades and adapting interiors. Thus the Victorian Gothic Cotton Exchange in Preston is now a cinema, the Round House in London a theater, the Gothic Temple at Stowe a holiday house. Faneuil Hall in Boston, Ghirardelli Square in San Francisco, and most recently Covent Garden in London now house smart boutiques and expensive restaurants. These conversion projects at best enhance the visual character of townscapes, providing a welcome alternative to the logos of fast food chains and gas stations. At worst, they become shopping malls for the prosperous, capitalist extravaganzas for the man and woman of taste.

The much-publicized birth of Post-Modernist architecture also testifies to the contemporary appropriation of the past. The pioneers of modern design and their advocates, of course, condemned nineteenth-century architectural historicism, praising only those structures, such as the Crystal Palace, that foreshadowed their own ideals. But those who live by revision eventually die by revision. Criticizing Modernist steel-and-glass boxes has become a popular pastime these days as architects turn upon their former teachers, not to mention their former

selves. Whereas history was a nightmare from which the Modernists tried to awaken, it provides visions Post-Modernists attempt to recapture. Those practitioners who have been found guilty of the "crime of ornament" have been paroled in a new architectural language derived from diverse historic idioms. Historicist buildings of the nineteenth and early twentieth centuries, notably the work of Edwin Lutyens, have not lacked admirers. They are appreciated increasingly, however, as something more than quaint articles from an old curiosity shop peddling the higher nostalgia. Post-Modernist architects and critics find historic styles exciting because they have alerted them to the value of vernacular traditions, regional associations, and aesthetic eclecticism.

Although I did not write this book to furnish a historical perspective on these contemporary enthusiasms, it may help interested readers to do precisely that. Preservers who read my accounts of the campaigns to save Kirkstall Abbey, Leeds, and the city churches of York will surely recognize problems they confront in their own work. Among these are the strength of private-property interests, the desire for "progress" through urban renewal, the high price of preservation, as well as indifference to the aesthetic worth and symbolic meanings of historic buildings. Yet they will recognize at the same time that unlike their Victorian predecessors, they can rely in many cases on governmental protection of historic sites. They will also observe that their projects to salvage and rehabilitate entire districts are far more ambitious than the necessarily more modest plans of their Victorian counterparts.

In the course of writing this book I have incurred many debts. For their unfailing courtesy and assistance I am grateful to the staffs of the Bradford Central Reference Library, the Bradford Historical and Antiquarian Society, the British Library, Chetham's Library, the Guildhall Library, the Jesus College, Oxford, Library, the Manchester Central Reference Library, the Manchester Town Hall, the Royal Institute of British Architects, the Society for the Protection of Ancient Buildings, the Sussex

Archaeological Society, the Victoria and Albert Museum, and the Yorkshire Archaeological Society. My special thanks to Mrs. Monica Dance, former secretary of the Society for the Protection of Ancient Buildings. I am grateful to Mrs. Elizabeth Moore of *The Illustrated London News*, Mr. Michael Seaborne of the Museum of London, Mr. Stephen Croad of the National Monuments Record, and Mr. Ralph Hyde of the Guildhall Library for help in selecting illustrations. For permission to quote from manuscripts in their possession, I am grateful to the Society for the Protection of Ancient Buildings, the Sussex Archaeological Society, and the City of Manchester Cultural Services Department. Yale University's Concilium on International Studies awarded me a fellowship that enabled me to undertake the research for this book, and the College of Liberal Arts at Arizona State University helped defray the cost of illustrations. Mrs. Ruth Bardrick, Mrs. Raedine Price, and Ms. Cathleen Mullins typed the manuscript accurately and cheerfully. I would like to thank my father-in-law, Ralph Homa, for his aid in obtaining illustrations. The friendship and hospitality of Sarena Joseph, Peter Petzal, and Daniella Douek in London made the writing of much of this book all the more pleasurable.

It is fitting that a book that explores the English infatuation with the past be published by Cambridge, which is the world's oldest university press. At Cambridge I am particularly indebted to Steven Fraser for his early commitment to this work and for his patience in awaiting its completion and to Frank Smith for his sensitive editing and tactful suggestions.

Although it is now fashionable to analyze the "anxiety of influence," the intellectual influences on me have been a source of pleasure and instruction. Norman F. Cantor, my undergraduate mentor, bears much of the responsibility for my having become a professional historian in the first place. He taught me, among other things, the importance of interrelating intellectual and social history. I owe him thanks for the suggestion to write on medievalism and for his aid in helping me do so. Franklin Le Van Baumer advised the Yale University History Department dissertation on which this book is based with

critical rigor and good humor. He too suggested that I write on medievalism and helped turn an overly ambitious plan for a comparative study into a manageable subject. He encouraged me to be a self-starter and skillfully corrected my false starts. Asa Briggs helped me understand R. H. Tawney's dictum that every historian needs a good pair of boots, by emphasizing the need to see firsthand the places and objects I studied. He stressed the need to develop one's individuality while immersing oneself in the sources; to exploit visual as well as literary materials in order to make the past speak. He guided my work at every turn. I am grateful to these men for their insightful comments on the manuscript and for their continual kindness and encouragement.

I also want to thank Frank M. Turner for his excellent suggestions on an earlier draft of this book. I am sorry that I was unable to use his admirable study *The Greek Heritage in Victorian Britain* while completing my own work. (The same holds true for Mark Girouard's *The Return to Camelot: Chivalry and the English Gentlemen* and J. W. Burrow's *A Liberal Descent: Victorian Historians and the English Past*.) Peter Gay, John Clive, Carl Schorske, Arno Mayer, Owen Chadwick, R. B. Pugh, E. V. Walter, John F. Stephens, and Joel Goldberg all made useful suggestions. Steven Mintz helped sharpen the ideas in this book from its first prospectus to its final chapter. As usual, I alone am responsible for the shortcomings that remain.

Let me finally thank my parents, my wife, and my brothers, not least for tolerating me as I worked on this book. It is dedicated to my mother and father for their unflagging emotional and financial support; for teaching me the love of learning; and for believing in me when it was difficult to believe in myself. For this and much else I am profoundly grateful.

Charles Dellheim

The paradoxes of progress

Railway termini and hotels are to the nineteenth
century what monasteries and cathedrals were to
the thirteenth century. They are truly the only real
representative building we possess.
                        – *Building News* (1875)

The pointed arch and the iron horse

The conspicuous presence of Gothic railway stations in the
nineteenth century dramatizes a fundamental paradox of Victorian culture: fascination with the medieval inheritance in
the age of progress. In historic towns like Bristol and industrial towns like Middlesbrough, in the provinces as well as in
the metropolises, medieval modes were used to construct what
Victorians saw as their representative building. There is little
in the bold asymmetry or exuberant silhouette of London's St.
Pancras (1867–74), for example, to announce that it is neither
a cathedral nor a cloth hall but a railway hotel now used as an
office building.[1] The irony implicit in the unexpected union of
the pointed arch and the iron horse may stand as an emblem
of a broader enigma. Dr. Thomas Arnold may have believed
that the advent of the railway signaled the "death of feudal-
ity," but in fact there was no intrinsic contradiction between
the pursuit of technological progress and the rehabilitation of
historic forms; the medievalized facade and the modern interior of St. Pancras are two faces of the same medal. The architecture of the Gothic railway station suggests that if the concern
with the Middle Ages was, on the one hand, a protest against
industrial society, on the other hand it became an integral
part of its culture, because it satisfied the longing for continuity without impeding the march of improvement.

The fascination with history embodied in the Gothic railway station was no more limited to Britain than confined to

*St. Pancras Railway
Station and Hotel, circa
late nineteenth century.
(By permission of the
National Monuments
Record.)*

the medieval world. It manifested itself in nineteenth-century Europe in the proliferation of historical studies, the vogue of the historical novel, the building of museums, the growth of tourism, the study of natural history, and, most visibly, in the triumph of architectural historicism. No single time or place preoccupied the European imagination; indeed, it was wildly eclectic, finding inspiration and guidance mainly in classical Greece and Rome, Medieval Europe, and Renaissance Italy. The historical problem posed by these phenomena is why the concern with the past flourished in an increasingly industrial,

2

St. Pancras Railway
Station shed, circa 1895.
(By permission of the
National Monuments
Record.)

progressive society. This book attempts to illuminate this cultural paradox by exploring the encounter with the medieval legacy in Victorian England. It focuses, in short, on medievalism in modernity. "Medievalism" here means the appeal to, and the appeal of, the artifacts, styles, and institutions of Europe from approximately the fifth to the fifteenth centuries. "Modernity" here means the industrial, technological civilization devoted to the development of science, the celebration of the individual, and the pursuit of political and economic freedom.[2]

The rediscovery of the Middle Ages did not begin, of course, with the Victorians. For a small band of highly cultivated and

3

equally eccentric upper-class Augustan amateurs such as Horace Walpole, Batty Langley, and Sanderson Miller, medieval architectural forms and literary themes provided an escape from the limitations of a rationalistic culture. Gothic architecture furnished the basis for an aesthetic that satisfied their desire for asymmetry, wildness, variety, and movement. Far from defining "nature" in terms of balance, harmony, and regularity, they turned to Gothic as an exemplar of the grotesque, the exotic, and the sublime.[3] The artists and thinkers of the Romantic movement were the heirs of this tradition insofar as they were attracted to the Middle Ages because of its romance and color, heroism and beauty — qualities they often found wanting in contemporary life. What is new in their approach to the past is that they saw in the Middle Ages a source of values that represented alternatives to the emergent industrial capitalist social order. In Gothic architecture they saw the highest expression of the human quest for the infinite and delight in the finite. The Middle Ages provided them with an exemplar of spiritual certainty and religious piety that was profoundly appealing to those who craved both but often possessed neither. Chivalry, feudalism, and the guild — these medieval forms served as animating ideals for those alarmed by the cash-nexus of industrial capitalism.[4]

Victorians also invoked the Middle Ages to criticize their own times, but this was only one face of Victorian medievalism. Their fascination with the Middle Ages manifests itself in a wide range of cultural artifacts. The novels of Walter Scott and Edward Bulwer-Lytton; the Arthurian romances of Alfred Tennyson, William Morris, and Algernon Swinburne; the mythological and historical paintings of Dante Gabriel Rossetti and Edward Burne-Jones; the histories of Edward Freeman, J. R. Green, and William Stubbs; the Gothic Revival in secular and ecclesiastical architecture; all these testify to the vogue of medievalism. Many of England's finest writers, artists, architects, and reformers turned to the medieval past in seeking sources for their poetry and novels, models for their buildings, a basis for political dogma, and an antidote to the ills of mod-

ern life. Other Victorians also venerated the Middle Ages. There they found the crucible in which provincial and national identities had been forged, an exemplar of aesthetic values as well as national symbols worthy of preservation. It is also notable that for all the social changes they engineered, Victorians carefully preserved, indeed venerated, medieval institutions such as Parliament and the monarchy itself. And it was no accident that it was the Victorians who invented a new family of words including "mediaeval," "mediaevally," "mediaevalist," and "mediaevalize."[5] "Mediaeval" reflects awareness of the Middle Ages as a distinctive civilization with unique ideals and customs. "Mediaevalize" refers to the penchant for imitating and restoring aspects of medieval life and art as well as to the belief that they could be used to inform the present. And "mediaevalist" documents both the devotion to medieval ideals and the professionalization of medieval studies. Those Victorians who confidently announced the end of the Middle Ages were partly correct. But their prediction proved as premature as the prophecies of those who have predicted the demises of capitalism, the bourgeoisie, the family, and the novel, all of which have been on their respective deathbeds for centuries.

Victorians found many aspects of their lives colored by medievalism. In their childhoods the writings of Walter Scott created powerful images of the historic past and of the heroic life. Not simply historical novels but also the popular press, notably *The Illustrated London News*, which was founded in 1842, used visual as well as verbal media to describe the "Nooks and Crannies of Old England," such as Tintern Abbey and Pontefract Castle.[6] Another symptom of the widespread interest in the past was the vogue of sightseeing. Ecclesiologists devoted to the revival of medieval liturgy and architecture were not the only English people to admire medieval ecclesiastical remains. For instance, the Positivist Frederic Harrison was fascinated by the monastic ruins of Yorkshire, which he visited in 1845. Although he recognized that in the Middle Ages a "few real saints" were outnumbered by swarms of

The Houses of Parliament. (By permission of the Museum of London.)

"abominable ruffians," he was still transported by the vision of remnants that he associated with "times when men could live whole lives of unbroken repose and devotion." True, he inevitably entered cathedrals "with a very lively sense of the intense humbug it is now," but it is no less true that he became "quite maudlin in admiration of a Gothic church."[7]

The face of London was also medievalized during the nineteenth century. The most important event in this connection was the decision to construct the new Houses of Parliament in the Gothic style. Although it is ironic that by the time Sir Charles Barry and A. W. Pugin's creation was completed in 1860 its Perpendicular forms were unfashionable, nevertheless it legitimized the claims of Gothic to be the English national style. If the new Palace of Westminster was the greatest example of Victorian Gothic, churches were easily the most numerous and visible, because religious revivalists quickly

6

preempted Gothic's ecclesiastical associations. Among the Neo-Gothic churches that pervaded London were George Gilbert Scott's St. Clement, St. Clement's Street, Islington (1863–5); William Butterfield's All Saints, Margaret Street, Marylebone (1849–59); George Edmund Street's St. James, Sussex Gardens, Paddington (1881); Norman Pearson's St. Augustine, Kilburn Park Road, Kilburn (1870–80).

Nowhere is the changing visual identity of London more apparent than in the City. Its narrow streets and picturesque names betrayed their medieval origins long after the Great Fire of 1666 had destroyed all but a few of its original buildings. The central area of the City was largely rebuilt in the third quarter of the nineteenth century. During this period Gothic made considerable inroads in the commercial architecture of the mercantile citadel even though the classic style and its Italian grandchild still predominated.[8] Near the en-

*The Holborn Viaduct
under construction, circa
1869. (By courtesy of the
Guildhall Library, City
of London.)*

trance to the City stood George Edmund Street's "magnificent pile," the Law Courts (1874–82). Within the City's one square mile were the following Neo-Gothic buildings. At the Holborn Viaduct there were four Florentine Gothic houses designed by William Heywood, the city surveyor (1863–9). Moving along Newgate Street into Cheapside, on Poultry there was a late-Georgian brick house to whose upper floors R. W. Moore had added Gothic arcading (1869), as well as Mappin & Webb's Department Store (1870), designed by J. and J. Belcher.

Mansion House and Cheapside, including Mappin & Webb. (By permission of the Museum of London.)

Proceeding north along Ironmonger's Lane one would pass by No. 19 Basinghall Street, a Tuscan Gothic building with a glass front, and the Guildhall Free Library and Museum, built by Sir Horace Jones (1873), en route to the original medieval Guildhall, where J. Durham's Gothic drinking fountain (1886) stood. Returning to Poultry and heading east one would pass by No. 81 Cornhill, a Venetian Gothic front on the way to Bishopsgate. There one might inspect a Gothic fire station by George Vuillamy (1885), Barclay's Bank (1894), and Provident Association (1889) before coming to another of London's Gothic railway stations, Liverpool Street, the work of Edward Wilson (1875). Winding back Bishopsgate to Eastcheap one could not help but notice R. L. Roumieu's monument to medievalist excess: a gabled Gothic factory, of red and blue brick, designed

9

Liverpool Street Railway Station, circa 1890. (By permission of Guildhall Library, City of London.)

for a firm of vinegar manufacturers near Alfred Waterhouse's striking Clydesdale and North of Scotland Bank (1880) on Lombard Street. Farther east was the Tower Bridge (1886), which was sponsored by the City though it lay, strictly speaking, outside its limits. What is most significant about this route is that it demonstrates that the face of the City was more "medieval" in 1900 than it had been at any time since 1666. Where the remnants of the past had largely vanished, the Victorians resolutely manufactured architectural surrogates.

Warehouse, in Eastcheap. Engraving from The Builder, *1868. (By permission of the Guildhall Library, City of London.)*

*Clydesdale Bank, 1903.
(By permission of the
Guildhall Library, City
of London.)*

The varieties of medievalism

Medievalism was, therefore, a pervasive part of the world of the Victorians. But their relationship to the medieval past was ambivalent: On the one hand, many Victorians wanted to eliminate what they saw as the vestiges of feudalism; on the other, they were fascinated by medieval motifs, themes, and symbols. There was no single reason for their attraction to the Middle Ages. For some, medievalism was a regressive escape from the harsh realities of an intolerable world. For others, it was a decorative screen that concealed the workings of mass production and modern technology. For still others, it was an aesthetic backdrop that provided picturesque scenery and intense emotions.

Medieval institutions took on new meaning and relevance because of the social dislocations caused by rapid industrialization. By the early Victorian years, the medieval revival in politics, art, and religion was already well under way, as the following works demonstrate: A. W. Pugin's *Contrasts; or a Parallel between the Noble Edifices of the Middle Ages, and*

Gothic survival and revival: the Tower of London and Tower Bridge, circa 1920. (By permission of the Museum of London.)

13

Gothic interior: City Council Chambers, Guildhall, circa 1890. (By courtesy of the Guildhall Library, City of London.)

Corresponding Buildings of the Present Day, Shewing the Present Decay of Taste (1835); S. T. Coleridge's *On the Constitution of Church and State* (1836); Thomas Carlyle's *Past and Present* (1843); Benjamin Disraeli's *Sybil* (1845), and John Ruskin's *The Stones of Venice* (1851–3). What is most telling about these works is their humane vision, their recognition of the savagery of progress. Their authors turned to the Middle Ages not as dispassionate observers but as modern pilgrims in search of solutions to contemporary problems. These problems included the "birth of class" and the ensuing threat of social catastrophe; the "abdication of the governors" and the loss of effective, responsible leadership; the introduction of the factory system and the consequent division of labor, which resulted in the alienation of workers and the loss of craftsmanship; the triumph of egoism, self-interest, and exploitation in the name of laissez-faire individualism; the lukewarm piety and social insensitivity of the Church of England and its lack of ritual dignity and sacred mystery; the aesthetic confusion and visual ugliness of the industrial world. These symptoms of social disintegration were, in their view, the price paid for the repudiation of medieval traditions.[9]

Social critics turned to the medieval world because of the meanings they discerned in and attached to it. The Middle Ages served as a symbol of the world they had lost. Medievalist writers presented a highly idealized vision of medieval society as an exemplar of piety and faith, of just prices and good craftsmanship, of reciprocal responsibility and heroic leadership, of unequaled aesthetic achievement and visual splendor. By emphasizing the achievements of the Middle Ages they were able to expose and deflate the inadequacies and pretensions of the modern world. Not only did the past provide them with a foil, but it also furnished them with symbols that served as animating ideals. Of these the most important were the monastery, the Gothic cathedral, the feudal system, the chivalric code, the craftsman, and the guild. William Cobbett hoped to restore the high standard of living of laborers along with the ancient "rights of Englishmen." A. W. Pugin hoped to restore the unity of faith and purpose that was the

foundation of Gothic architecture. John Manners hoped to restore the harmonious community in which feudal lords motivated by chivalric ideals superintended the welfare of obedient peasants. Thomas Carlyle hoped to restore the union of authority and charity he saw in the Abbey of St. Edmund's as a defense against the freedom and dehumanization of a cash-nexus society. John Ruskin and William Morris hoped to restore the joy in labor, freedom, and craftsmanship of the medieval artisan to his machine-dominated modern counterpart.

Judging on the basis of their works, one would conclude that medievalism was a form of antimodern dissent. It was promulgated by and, for the most part, appealed to members of the landed elite, who feared that the new prominence of the industrial middle class would destroy their social position and cultural values, and social critics dissatisfied by the utilitarian ethos of an increasingly rationalistic, mechanical society. The solution to these problems was either to create a neofeudal society based on a paternalistic alliance between the upper and lower classes or to turn to socialism and thus eradicate oppressive class distinctions.

Yet medievalism was not the unchallenged cultural property of English conservatives. For centuries, progressive forces had invoked aspects of the Middle Ages to support their causes. According to the "Norman yoke" theory, before 1066 the Saxons lived as free and equal citizens with representative institutions. The Norman Conquest proved disastrous because it installed an alien king and landlords who destroyed the "ancient liberties" of the people. The "Norman yoke" served as a rallying cry for different groups in different periods: seventeenth-century Levellers used it to subvert existing "property rights"; eighteenth-century Radicals used it to destroy the historic arguments of Edmund Burke and to challenge the legitimacy of the monarchy and the peerage; nineteenth-century Radicals used it to support their quest for political and social democracy.[10] This vision of history also influenced English Liberals like Edward Freeman, J. R. Green, and James Bryce, who appealed to the Middle Ages to support their political values. This does not mean, of course, that all progressives turned to

the Middle Ages any more than all conservatives. The point is that medievalism had diverse forms and functions.

The career of Edward Freeman is of particular interest because it embodies the diverse strains of Victorian medievalism. Born in 1823 into the ranks of the Tory, Anglican gentry, he was influenced by the tail end of the Oxford movement during his time as a scholar at Trinity College. He became an active member of the Oxford Architectural Society, played an important part in their restoration of the famous Abbey Church of Dorchester, and later published an important treatise on *The Principles of Church Restoration* (1845). He joined the Brotherhood of St. Mary, a group devoted to the study of "ecclesiastical art upon true and Catholic principles," but withdrew when the organization became primarily religious. He seriously considered becoming an Anglican priest, but he did not do so because he believed himself unsuited to the required vow of celibacy.[11] Instead he turned to historical and architectural studies.

Like his hero William Gladstone, Freeman the ardent Tory became a dedicated Liberal. Although it is difficult to determine how and why his political opinions and ideals changed, it is probable that his study of Saxon history was a decisive factor.[12] Whatever the causes, he became a committed democrat and ran for Parliament as a Liberal in Cardiff in 1857, Wallingford in 1859, and Somerset in 1868, each time without success. His failure to win a seat in what he called, significantly, "the ancient Witan of England" was always a profound disappointment to him.[13] Unable to work for Liberal causes in Westminster, he did so through his historical writings.

Victorians could have created the term "mediaevalist" to suit Edward Freeman. An authority on the Middle Ages who also wrote extensively on classical and comparative history, he approached the past by touring visual survivals as well as by reading traditional sources. Though largely self-trained himself, he called for the professionalization of history and had little regard for antiquarians, whom he called a "feeble folk everywhere."[14] At the same time, he was a medievalist in that his historical work legitimized his Liberal political principles.

The man who firmly believed that politics and history were always influencing each other saw no contradiction between the two faces of his medievalism.

Freeman's *The Growth of the English Constitution* (1870) exemplifies how Liberals appropriated the Middle Ages to fabricate a viable political tradition. Its premise was that "the earliest institutions of England and of other Teutonic lands are not mere matters of curious speculation, but matters closely connected with our present being."[15] Its point was to demonstrate that the "holders of Liberal principles in modern politics need never shrink from tracing our political history to its earliest beginnings. As far at least as our race is concerned, freedom is everywhere older than bondage."[16] Following the example of Whigs from Edward Coke to J. M. Kemble, he carefully traced the genealogy of English liberty to the free world of the Anglo-Saxon forests described by Tacitus. The central symbol of the work was the "mark," the village community in which face-to-face democracy flourished – an ideal that Freeman hoped to revive. His basic tactic was to emphasize the organic character of English history, the "growth" of the English Constitution. By demonstrating that growth did not necessarily lead to disruption, he showed that "we can, therefore, reform without destroying."[17] He pictured democracy as the fulfillment of, and a return to, an ancient Teutonic tradition rather than as a foreign transplant. Thus, Freeman challenged conservatives on their own favored battleground and turned tradition on its head to justify, not invalidate, reform. More than one party saw its image in the deep well of the past.

The search for respectable pedigrees was a common feature of the Victorian cultural style. Liberals and conservatives alike legitimized their causes by invoking medieval symbols. That both critics and celebrants of modernity preempted medieval models suggests that for the Victorians, the Middle Ages provided a testing ground where they debated the kind of world they wanted to build as well as by what justification they would build it. Their medievalism, therefore, was essentially modern in the sense that it was concerned with contemporary

dilemmas. The fact that both the eulogists of tradition and the advocates of innovation derived master images from the Middle Ages highlights the inadequacy of analyzing medievalism simply in terms of antimodern dissent or promodern affirmation. These categories obscure a fundamental reality of nineteenth-century life: Conservatives had to adapt to an industrial, progressive society just as liberals had to cope with the world they had created.

Perspectives on a problem

Scholarly interest in medievalism dates back to Charles Eastlake's *A History of the Gothic Revival* (1872), the work of a partisan, if not uncritical, supporter of the movement he documented. He set the tone for later scholarship in his emphasis on medievalism as an episode in the history of architectural, artistic, and, to a lesser extent, literary taste. The classic account of this subject was written by Kenneth Clark, like Eastlake at one time a high official of the National Gallery, but unlike Eastlake an anti-Victorian rebel who had little sympathy with the products of the Gothic Revival. His essay *The Gothic Revival: An Episode in the History of Taste* (1928) interrelates the vogue of Gothic architecture with the rediscovery of Shakespeare and Milton, the fashion of antiquarianism and archeology, and the regeneration of Christian piety. His concern was with the ideals and motives of Gothic revivalists from Walpole to Ruskin and not primarily with the analysis of specific architectural and literary works. Recent scholarly inquiry has examined particular facets of eighteenth- and nineteenth-century medievalism, revising or amplifying the overview established by Eastlake and Clark. Alice Chandler's *A Dream of Order: The Medieval Ideal in Nineteenth Century English Literature* (1971) uses close textual analysis to illuminate the vision of the Middle Ages held by writers from Scott to Henry Adams, stressing their longing for a harmonious, hierarchical, ordered society. James F. White's *The Cambridge Movement: The*

Ecclesiologists and the Gothic Revival (1962) analyzes how the imitation and restoration of medieval architecture and liturgy expressed the aspirations of Anglican revivalists.

Yet for the general historian key questions remain unanswered. Architectural historians have been concerned, naturally, with the work of individual architects and schools as well as with questions of style and technique. Valuable as their work has been, their predominantly formalist approach neglects the fact that buildings are cultural artifacts as well as works of art.[18] There has been ample work done on such great monuments of the Gothic Revival as the Houses of Parliament, but the social and political significance of their iconography has not been attended to sufficiently. Historic restoration has also been scrutinized considerably, but research has not focused on what the treatment of architectural survivals reveals about Victorian attitudes toward the past. Treating medievalism as a set of aesthetic tastes and religious ideals is, of course, both valid and significant; yet it should not obscure the fact that medievalism was a widespread cultural phenomenon. It is certainly true that scholars have been aware of vernacular medievalism in the provinces, but thus far they have stressed the works of an elite of artists and thinkers, located along the London–Oxford–Cambridge axis. The time has come for a change in scope.

Many writers have asserted or implied that the Victorians' concern with the Middle Ages was a reaction against conditions in their own times. E. P. Thompson argued that medievalism was a protest against the values and realities of the new industrial, capitalist society.[19] This is undoubtedly an important insight, amply substantiated by a subtle reading of the works of Carlyle, Ruskin, and Morris. Yet it underplays the fact that medieval artifacts and styles appealed to many Victorians not in revolt against modern civilization. If Victorian medievalism was, as Thompson argues, only a "revolt against the world of the Railway Age and the values of Gradgrind," how then can one explain the existence of Gothic railway stations or the spate of buildings in the north of England sponsored by the alleged heirs of Gradgrind?

Certainly historians recognized previously that medievalism was more than antimodern dissent. E. P. Thompson's study of William Morris contains suggestive ideas concerning the appeal of medieval culture to Morris's circle of friends at Oxford, many of whom came from industrial Birmingham. Asa Briggs illuminated the symbiosis between medievalism and modernity exemplified by the medieval court at the Great Exhibition of 1851.[20] And it is well known that progressive forces traditionally appealed to the Middle Ages, notably to the Magna Charta and the "Norman yoke," to support their calls for change. One aim of the present study is to extend and elaborate these insights. It is not an attempt to invalidate the view that medievalism was a protest against industrial capitalism but instead to underline the complexities of the Victorians' uses of the past.

The perspective I adopt in this book is to examine medievalism as an example of the recovery of the past and not simply as an end in itself. The cultural activities analyzed here all reflect the general concern with history, as the following examples suggest. Yorkshire archeologists who discovered a number of ancient coins would not have valued them any less had they been Roman rather than Norman, any more than Sussex tourists' love of medieval castles would have prevented them from admiring the ruins of Stonehenge. Certain members of the Society for the Protection of Ancient Buildings might have been interested especially in saving medieval churches, yet at the same time they campaigned to protect Elizabethan architecture. If many Victorians were devoted, indeed fanatical, Goths, others were no less dedicated Classicists. What is perhaps more significant than the celebrated "battle of the styles" is the penchant for architectural eclecticism, combining features of various styles in a single building or using different styles for different building types. A. W. Pugin remarked, for instance, that the Houses of Parliament were "all Grecian, . . . Tudor details on a Classic body." Although I cannot in this book examine all the faces of the concern with the past, I do try to examine medievalism in a broad context. Hence, the Victorians' encounter with England's

21

medieval past receives the spotlight but does not occupy the entire stage.

Historians are at the mercy of their sources just as the sources are all too often at the mercy of historians. To understand the broad dimension of Victorian attitudes toward the past, it is necessary to move beyond the artifacts of high culture to a diverse range of visual and verbal sources. In this book I have, therefore, drawn upon manuscripts as well as printed sources rarely mined. The journals and archives of county archeological and historical societies revealed what aspects of the past interested Victorians. The membership lists of these groups in industrial and nonindustrial regions offered glimpses into who was interested in the past. Excursion and tourist literature provided information on how Victorians responded to historic survivals and how they related them to their modern settings. Innumerable local histories and guidebooks were the sources of insights into the associations that people gave to specific places and the myths they derived from history. Popular histories of England showed how Victorians interpreted specific events, what figures were important to them, and how they related the past to the present. The professional journals of architects, the archives of preservationist societies, the reporting of local newspapers revealed diverse conceptions of what people thought should be done with medieval buildings, their ideals of restoration and preservation, as well as the actual social dynamics that shaped the fate of buildings. Municipal architecture and records provided documentation about the construction of Neo-Gothic buildings and about how medieval materials and forms were accommodated to the demands of the present.

The method I chose to analyze these materials was to use a series of "cross sections," as Jacob Burckhardt called them, that focus on particular facets of the Victorians' encounter with their inheritance. The studies in this book emphasize general cultural activities rather than high culture; secular rather than ecclesiastical attitudes; the middle rather than the upper or lower class; the provinces rather than London; the second rather than the first half of the nineteenth century. I

explore the face of the past from three interrelated angles. I begin by examining how Victorians in different regions, industrial and nonindustrial, perceived the visual survivals of the past, exploring how their investigations merged with the quest for provincial and national identities. Then I turn to attempts to restore and preserve medieval remains and how the fate of these survivals was affected by a variety of social, economic, religious, and aesthetic considerations. I end by examining how Victorians rehabilitated medieval architectural styles to construct buildings that met contemporary functional requirements, creating at the same time a sense of the past.

Throughout I rely on case studies, because they allow the historian to capture the atmosphere of the age, the texture of experience, and the contingency of events; to determine who put forth particular ideals and values, what functions they served, and how they fit into the web of social relations. The question case studies inevitably raise is whether they are representative; and to this there is no clear-cut response. Clifford Geertz pointed out that it is a fallacy to suppose that one can discover the essence of societies in "typical" villages or towns. Far from being "America writ small," Jonesville, alas, is only Jonesville.[21] Matters have become more complicated still as historical research on the social structures, economies, and cultures of different places and regions reveals their distinctiveness. It has, therefore, become increasingly dangerous and difficult to demonstrate that individual cases are representative.

Given these difficulties it is particularly important to state explicitly the criteria by which specific cases were selected. The first criteria I used was the symbolic significance of an example. Of the many Neo-Gothic public buildings erected in the Victorian age, I chose to focus on the making of the Manchester Town Hall because it best illustrated the general theme that medievalism was part and parcel of the industrial world. The second criterion I used was that the cases had to be sufficiently well documented to permit intensive, microcosmic examination. It is relatively easy in many instances to determine the fate of particular medieval architectural survivals in Victorian England. It is more difficult, and to my mind more

rewarding, to explore what Victorians felt and thought about the remains in their midst. The stories of the battles to save Kirkstall Abbey, Leeds, and the city churches of York may or may not be representative of all such campaigns. But they provide invaluable glimpses into Victorian values and attitudes as well as the forces that shaped the politics of preservation. The third criterion I used was regional diversity. I tried to study cultural activities in industrial and nonindustrial cities and counties alike. Yet I would not claim that this is a comprehensive survey that includes all types of localities. Much remains to be said about "preindustrial industrial centers" with a continuous past, like Nottingham, and, above all, about London. Finally, I attempt to set individual case studies in their general context. Thus, the discussion of local archeological societies focuses on Sussex and Yorkshire, but it does so only after establishing the pervasiveness of such organizations.

The functions of tradition

The fascination with the past was not, of course, a unique feature of nineteenth-century culture; it has been a recurrent, if not universal, theme of Western history.[22] All people are, for better or worse, their own historians by virtue of having a memory that records, deletes, and organizes their experiences. In order to understand the Victorians' encounter with their legacy, it is necessary to consider the general social functions of the past.

The "past" is not merely a haphazard collection of events and stories, historical and legendary. Raymond Williams argued that we experience the past as "tradition." If tradition is on the one hand simply the surviving past, it is on the other hand a selective version of the past that highlights certain meanings and practices while omitting, diluting, or neglecting others. The fabrication of a tradition out of the rich materials of the past is, in the broadest sense, a political process related to the establishment and maintenance of hegemony. It

reflects the interests and aspirations of a ruling elite who interpret the past in their image to ratify their values and connect with their world. They base their legitimacy, in part, on their role as proprietors of the past: By defining the "great tradition" of their society, they relegate competing ideals to the periphery. Yet tradition is not the exclusive preserve of dominant elites: It is also exhumed by their opponents. Dispossessed groups often turn to an idealized past as the basis for protests against their present condition and demands for the restitution of their lost "historic rights." Tradition can also serve the cause of new elites, who criticize the official version of the past as they appropriate distinguished pedigrees for themselves and their ideals. In their struggle for hegemony they reinterpret what constitutes the "significant past," rejecting or enlarging the current "great tradition," rediscovering aspects of the past that legitimize their ideology and style of life. Entrenched elites respond to such challenges by reaffirming "traditional values" just as their utility and justice are questioned.[23]

The role of tradition is different, however, in premodern and modern societies. Premodern societies are "traditional" in their acceptance of the sanctity of a historic individual, event, or order; in their commitment to historic symbols and customs; in their acceptance of the past as a basic source of collective identity; in their reference to the past as a prescriptive force dictating cultural norms; and in their legitimation of innovation in terms of the customs of the past.[24] The past, in brief, provides the pattern of life for the present; it is, in Eric Hobsbawm's phrase, "the court of appeal for present disputes." Because there is no conception of continuous progress, fundamental cultural and religious changes are seen as "restorations," returns to an aspect of tradition that has been neglected or corrupted, rather than as innovations.[25]

S. N. Eisenstadt argued that although the functions of tradition change in modern societies, modernity is not traditionless. But modernization does make it socially desirable to reject historic ideals and institutions that retard progress. In so doing it inevitably raises two basic questions. The first is how to determine which tradition represents the true tradition of the

community given the conflicting versions of the past offered by different groups. The second question is how, and to what extent, it is possible to incorporate tradition into a new social framework. He argues that tradition survives in modernity through the reconstruction of its forms and functions. The "reconstruction of tradition" means that traditional and non-traditional spheres are segregated so that historic values are far more binding in certain spheres, such as religion, than in others, such as technology.[26] Thus, loyalty to the past need not impede the commitment to progress, and modernization need not mean the death of tradition.

In modernity, tradition becomes the proverbial coat of many colors, subtle shading, and varied owners. By stripping historic symbols of their conventional meanings, elites rehabilitate the past to glorify contemporary ideals and institutions. By incorporating aspects of tradition into a new society, the past furnishes alternative models to the life of the present. But here too the past is a double-edged tool: It can support backward-looking and forward-looking visions, infatuations with the archaic, as well as experiments with the unprecedented. If there is, strictly speaking, no escape from the present, the past provides an emotional refuge for those alienated from their own times. Yet it is also true that the exploration of the past, indeed its very presence, represents a way to cope with change. The present can be seen as organic development from the past rather than a radical departure from it.

One of the most striking manifestations of the concern with the past is the idea of restoration. Karl Marx argued in a famous passage of *The Eighteenth Brumaire of Louis Napoléon* (1852) that restorations are not mere revivals.

> The traditions of all the dead generations weigh like a nightmare on the brain of the living. And just when they seemed engaged in revolutionizing themselves and things, in creating something that has never yet existed, precisely in such periods of revolutionary crisis they anxiously conjure up the spirits of the past to their service and borrow from them names,

battle cries, and costumes in order to present the new scene of world history in this time-honored disguise and this borrowed language.[27]

Marx then offers as an explanation:

> Thus the awakening of the dead in those revolutions served the purpose of glorifying the new struggles, not of parodying the old; of magnifying the given task in imagination, not of fleeing from its solution in reality; of finding once more the spirit of revolution, not of making its ghost walk about again.[28]

Marx makes three crucial points here. The first is that "restorations" can be masks for innovation. The second is that revolutionaries as well as conservatives find animating ideals in the past. And the final point is that the concern with the past can express progressive as well as reactionary goals. All of these were true of Victorian England.

Victorians invoked, admired, and pillaged many traditions, but two conceptions of historical culture were preeminent in their minds. As Lord Acton put it, "Two great principles divide the world and contend for the mastery, antiquity and the middle ages." Like other grandiose pronouncements that split reality into two opposing principles, Acton's great divide was not as neat a border as he believed.[29] Neither territory was itself unitary: Different aspects of medieval and classical culture appealed to different Victorians for different reasons. Medievalism and classicism, for all their substantial differences, had certain common features. Both idealized preindustrial societies that represented clear alternatives to the contemporary world; and both expressed rural, pastoral fantasies as well as anticommercial and antimaterialist sentiments. It is tempting to categorize medievalists as devout Christians and classicists as happy pagans, yet Gladstone, for instance, was no less pious a follower of Christ for being so fanatical an admirer of Homer. It is tempting also to present classicists as ardent

republicans and medievalists as enthusiastic feudalists, but many admired medieval cities as crucibles of bourgeois liberty and classical Greece as an exemplar of aristocratic elitism. And, finally, the border between the Middle Ages and classical antiquity was never so tightly policed as to prevent certain Victorians, like E. A. Freeman, from indulging an interest in both.

Yet there were striking differences in the respective places of medievalism and classicism in Victorian culture. The classics provided the central core of the educational curriculum of the public schools and the ancient universities. Comparatively scant attention was paid to medieval studies, though its status improved after reforms in the History School at Oxford in the 1860s and the appointment of the great medievalist William Stubbs to the Regius Professorship of History there. Although the Camden Society, which was composed of Cambridge undergraduates and dons, had considerable influence in promoting the taste for medieval architecture and ritual, its impact on formal instruction at the University of Cambridge was peripheral. The study of the art and history of medieval England was carried on mainly in nonacademic settings – in local archeological and historical societies which, by the way, were also concerned with the artifacts of Roman England. The researches of these organizations expressed and enhanced provincial and national loyalties, whereas classical studies promoted universalist ideals, though they did so with an unmistakably British accent. The writings of Homer and Virgil, Horace and Cicero, furnished a pantheon of heroes and a grammar for living suitable for all, though available to few. The study of the local and national history of England, medieval and modern, was far more accessible to Victorians who had not received a classical education.

What is more relevant here than the forms of the cult of the past is why it flourished in an increasingly industrial, progressive world. The ambiguities of English social history help illuminate this apparent paradox. One key is that although England was the first nation to industrialize, it retained many characteristics of a status-oriented, hierarchical society based

on land and privilege, custom and convention.[30] This is not to
say that preindustrial ideals and institutions survived intact
or that their functions did not change, but only to stress their
persistence in a new setting. Walter Bagehot recognized that
deference was a fundamental ingredient of the Victorian social and political order. The aristocratic traditions of England
tempered the values of the business world. The "worship of
rank," whatever its intrinsic merits, ensured that England never
became dedicated solely to the "rule of wealth – the religion
of gold."[31] Deep into the century of progress, and in many
respects long thereafter, the landed aristocracy and gentry retained great wealth, power, and prestige. Karl Marx believed
that the middle class was a revolutionary force that would
overthrow aristocratic dominion, but in fact the middle class
often deferred to the aristocracy, accepting their right to exist
if not necessarily to rule. W. D. Rubinstein clarified the social
basis of deference with his argument that there were two middle classes in Victorian England: one based on wealth derived
from manufacturing, located in the provinces and especially
in the north; the other based on wealth derived from finance
and commerce, based in London or in mercantile centers like
Liverpool and Leeds.[32] The latter class had close ties to the
landed elite and hoped to join their number or, at the very
least, imitate their manner. Their path to assimilation into
the aristocracy was clearly marked, if not always easily followed: The main steps were purchasing a country estate, send-
ing one's sons to public schools to become gentlemen, if not
scholars, and marrying off one's daughters to one's betters.

The persistence of certain aspects of a status society that
cherished history, custom, and tradition helps to explain the
prestige of the past in the industrial world. The existence of
two middle classes sheds light on the different functions the
past assumed for different groups. Middle-class Victorians with
aristocratic pretensions and aspirations imitated the upper class's
display of historic paraphernalia. Because few financiers and
industrialists received peerages until the late-Victorian age,
those intent on assimilating into the aristocracy in the mid-
Victorian era had to content themselves with such surrogates

as coats of arms, heraldic devices, Gothic villas, and long pedigrees. Thomas Hardy parodied this social type in *Tess of the D'Urbervilles* (1891):

> When old Mr. Simon Stoke, latterly deceased, had made his fortune as an honest merchant (some said money-lender) in the North, he decided to settle as a county man in the South of England, out of hail of his business district; and in doing this he felt the necessity of recommencing with a name that would not too readily identify him with the smart tradesman of the past, and that would be less commonplace than the original bald stark words. Conning for an hour in the British Museum the pages of works devoted to extinct, half-extinct, obscured and ruined families appertaining to the quarter of England in which he proposed to settle, he considered that 'd'Urberville' looked and sounded as well as any of them: and d'Urberville accordingly was annexed to his own name for himself and his heirs eternally. Yet he was not an extravagant-minded man in this, and in constructing his family tree on the new basis was duly reasonable in framing his intermarriages and aristocratic links, never inserting a single title above a rank of strict moderation.[33]

This attitude was anathema to the liberal middle class. As they tried to reform the "old corruption," they naturally rejected the argument from tradition that supported aristocratic privilege. Richard Cobden and John Bright wanted to destroy the forms and spirit of feudalism, yet their Anti–Corn Law League speeches reveal that they identified with the struggle of the medieval burghers of the Hanseatic League against aristocratic tyranny. This suggests that they did not reject tradition per se, but only its aristocratic version and its reactionary uses. The liberal middle class accepted the aristocratic emphasis on antiquity only to subvert it by fabricating traditions that supported their own claims to legitimacy.

The role of the past in Victorian culture was in general neither prescriptive nor normative. The concern with history expressed both progressive and conservative values. The essential point is that Victorians reconstructed the past to create a cultural tradition that balanced progress and continuity. Reshaping traditions allowed them to forge connections with their history as they liberated themselves from its social, economic, and theological restraints. The artifacts, styles, and institutions of the Middle Ages that they idealized furnished symbolic surrogates for the world they had renounced. Yet these links to the past were bridges to the future more than detours from the present. How Victorians incorporated the survivals of their medieval inheritance into the first industrial society is our story.

2

The vision of history

The interest attaching to antiquity is of a very fascinating character. It is not limited to any locality or
epoch. It may be intensified by historical associations,
or localised by becoming centred upon any particular object; but speaking of it in its fullest...it is
illimitable...It may be that the antique of whatever
order, acquires a deeper halo in proportion as it may
be invested with the spirit of ages, just as the enthusiastic antiquary would leap for joy upon suddenly
unearthing a Roman denarius, while he might only
consider himself lucky in discovering a Queen Anne's
farthing.
– William Cudworth, *The Bradford Antiquary* (1888)

The visual encounter with the past

In 1845, the construction of a railway line in Sussex between
Hastings and Brighton necessitated passing through the small
town of Lewes. Thus, workers made an immense cut in the
earth near the site of the ruins of the Priory of St. Pancras, a
Cluniac monastery founded by William I soon after the Norman Conquest and largely destroyed by Cromwellian vandals
in 1638. When on 28 October 1845 a worker pushed his shovel
against a chest decorated with Caen stones, which he found
two feet from the surface, a bystander who had been hoping
that the excavations would uncover historic relics sent for the
local antiquarian Mark Antony Lower. As the latter brushed
the soil from the coffins, "great was the astonishment and
delight of the spectators" to find legibly inscribed on one the
name "Gundrada" and on the other the name "Willem." Soon
enough, Lower recognized that these were the remains of the
Norman founders of the Lewes Priory, William de Warenne
and his wife Gundrada.[1]

The great interest provoked by the unexpected discovery of
the bones of the Norman aristocrats exemplifies the fascina-

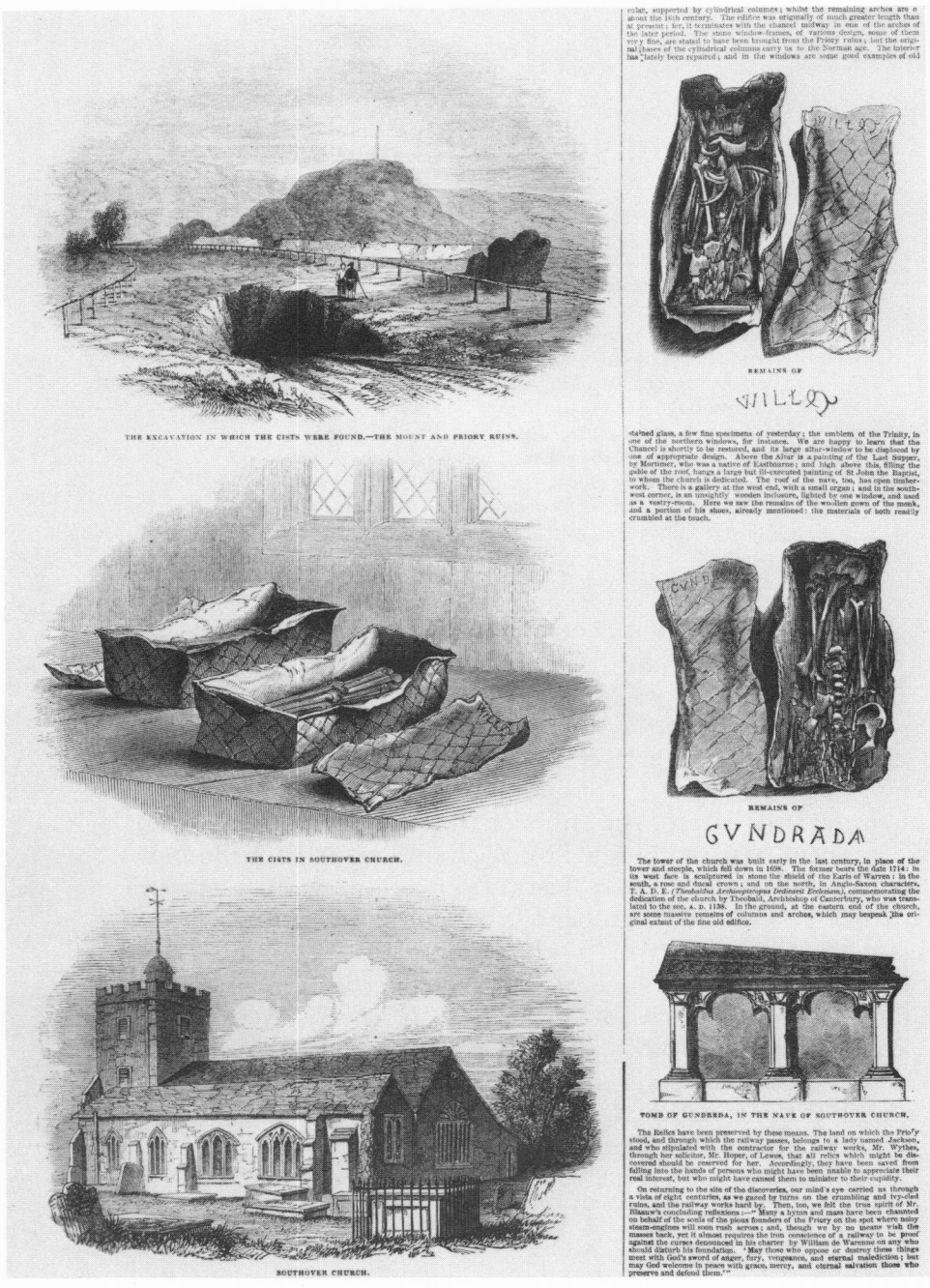

The discoveries at Lewes. From The Illustrated London News, *8 November 1845, p. 296. (By permission of* The Illustrated London News *Picture Library.)*

tion with medieval survivals in Victorian England. Delighted by the find, Mark Antony Lower, along with his fellow antiquarian W. H. Blaauw, did extensive research on the lives and genealogies of the nobles and on the ecclesiastical and architectural history of the monastery they founded; made arrangements for further excavations in the expectation of unearthing more antiquities; and laid the groundwork for the Sussex Archaeological Society, one of the first Victorian organizations of its kind.[2] They sent the remains of Gundrada and William to a local physician and surgeon, who concluded that the earl had been over six feet tall and the countess more than five and a half feet tall – formidable statures for medieval people.[3] The relics captured considerable popular as well as learned attention. The events in Lewes caught the eye of *The Illustrated London News*, whose editors sent a reporter to delve into the circumstances and background of the astounding discoveries and commissioned an artist to sketch the ruins and the remains for a one-page spread.[4] Whereas the "ruins until lately were a scene of melancholy decay, visited with interest by many a lover of antiquities but little heeded by the people of the neighbourhood," by the end of October 1845, the site was "covered with wonder-struck inquirers."[5]

The perfect irony of the situation – that the advent of the railway, the archetypal herald of progress, inadvertently led to the discovery of Norman relics – did not pass unnoticed by contemporaries. *The Illustrated London News*'s reporter, for instance, was struck by the curious commingling of the medieval and the modern. "Strange indeed," he commented, using language reminiscent of the Gothic novel, "are the changes wrought by time and man's ingenuity; for these relics of nearly eight centuries have been uprooted in a work peculiar to our own time – the construction of a railway; and this by a circumstance purely accidental, and but for which the relics might have rested for many centuries." His testimony also suggests that technological disruptions tended to highlight the presence of the relics of the medieval past: "On returning to the site of the discoveries our mind's eye carried us through a

vista of eight centuries, as we gazed by turns on the crumbling and ivy clad ruins and the railway-works nearby."[6]

Intriguing also are the various attitudes toward the medieval survivals. The question of how to treat them became the subject of a lively local debate whose flavor was distinctively Victorian. Some argued that it was a "pious duty" to return the "remains of our fellow creatures" to the earth for suitable burial, especially because exposing them to "public gaze" would most certainly shock many persons and make the archeologists appear irreligious.[7] Yet others, no less mindful of the religious obligations involved, had no "horror of their being seen," because the souls of the aristocrats had long since departed from their decayed bones.[8] Material as well as spiritual interests entered into the controversy and they eventually triumphed. The railway directors, frankly admitting that they regarded the matter with a "business eye," offered to lend every possible assistance in the excavations and to denote fifty pounds for a suitable receptacle for the relics, as long as they were assured that they would always be open to public view. Unlike a few of the archeologists, who hoped to push the masses back without discouraging their interest in the survivals, the directors hoped that the presence of the medieval remains would encourage tourists, particularly those on holiday in Brighton, to use the railway to inspect them in Lewes.[9] Their hope was fulfilled: Enough people visited Southover Church, where the relics were finally housed, and the ruins of the Priory of St. Pancras, where they had been discovered, to merit the publication of a guidebook and to justify Mark Antony Lower's boast – "Our town is rapidly rising with greater celebrity than it has ever yet enjoyed."[10]

Like any good Victorian story, the story of the discovery of medieval relics in Lewes has a moral, indeed several morals. The unexpected bounty of the iron horse convinced William Figg that the "common idea that railways are destructive in their tendencies and can be but of little use to archeaology or the arts" was simply wrong.[11] As often as not, the railway enjoyed a welcome reception because it brought new

life to sleepy towns even when it did not awaken, or at least, uncover, old bones. And the eagerness of the railway directors, as well as the people of Lewes, to capitalize on the antiquities reveals how the burgeoning interest in the past was commercialized in mass tourism.

Yet the story is most instructive in that it dramatically shows that medieval survivals, like those of other ages, were a physical presence in the improving, industrializing society of Victorian England. Anachronisms they surely were, but nonetheless they were as real as the railway and the factory. Like Thomas Hardy's Casterbridge, which "announced old Rome in every street, alley and precinct...looked Roman, bespoke the art of Rome, concealed dead men of Rome," the material world in which Victorians lived and worked still teemed with the remains of different eras of the past. These antiquities were fundamental to the sense of place.[12] Hence, for most Victorians the sense of the past was a visual rather than a verbal faculty, cultivated in the landscape more often than in the library, shaped in a direct encounter with material objects.

The Victorian sense of the past has to be understood in the context of the impact of industrialization and the social, economic, and technological processes associated with it. Although the events at Lewes just described suggest that it would be a mistake to posit all-embracing generalizations on so complex a matter as the relationship between social dislocations and historical consciousness, industrialization certainly affected the vision of history in at least two ways. By finally destroying many of the social structures and material remains of "olde England," it indirectly led to the idealization of the vanishing past. In so doing, it dramatized the distinctiveness of historic towns and relics. And by opening a huge chasm between the unprecedented world of the nineteenth century and the pre-industrial world, it shattered the chain of historic continuity and heightened the awareness of change.

When Victorians contemplated the different layers of time embodied in their landscapes and townscapes they were struck

by the contrast between the past and the present. In 1869, for example, a writer in the *Wakefield Express* recorded his impression of the vast gulf that separated medieval and modern society in his account of the visit of the Huddersfield Archaeological and Topographical Society to his town. Especially noteworthy is the "romantic" rhetoric of the following passages:

> Stretching east and west there lies almost beneath his feet the thriving town of Wakefield . . . with waving fields of golden corn studded here and there with towns and villages, the busy hives of manufacturing industry. A peaceful and prosperous scene, in strange contrast with the mouldering fragments of feudal grandeur which lie scattered on the ground below. No longer does the place resound with clang of arms, the tramp of horse, or the busy note of preparation for the coming fray; the warriors sleep beneath the sod, the lofty gateway, the grim and massive keep, the spacious banquet hall in which the feudal noble displayed his little less than regal splendour, are all swept away.[13]

His sense of the simultaneous pastness and presence of the past was linked to his awareness of the obliteration of numerous architectural artifacts that evoked images of the Yorkshire town's rich and glorious past.

> The destructive hand of man and the 'progress of the age', which respects not antiquity, nor regards historical associations, have, however, swept away many an object dear to the antiquarian, while the mouldering hand of time, slowly and silently, though nonetheless surely had added its share to the work of demolition. Of the many quaint old houses which the town a few years back contained, almost the last remaining is the venerable palatial structure known as the 'Six Chimneys', which still affords a specimen of our ancient domestic architecture, and as the beholder gazes on its curious carvings and overhanging

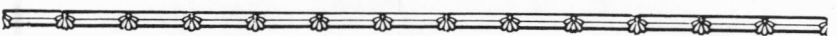

stories, the imagination again peopling the house with its olden inhabitants, wanders back to the 'good old times', three hundred years ago...Passed away also has the Ancient Market Cross, around which were wont to gather these prosperous genial trades-folk, and rendered memorable as the spot where the Royalists, in one of the many desperate fights of which the town was the scene...gone too has the old rectory, which for four hundred years was the residence of succeeding vicars of the merry town; perished also, by the hand of time, has the venerable class tree with all its romantic associations and historic traditions of the house of Maude.[14]

The ruination and disappearance of countless remains of different eras of the English past – Roman, Saxon, Norman, Elizabethan – enhanced the value, interest, and fascination of those relics that survived, "stranded in a distant age...like fragments of a shipwreck."

Nowhere is the visual character of the Victorian sense of the past more strikingly evident than in the popularity of historical and archeological sightseeing. Not content with letting antiquities, as it were, find them, Victorians actively sought the survivals of the preindustrial past, especially those of Roman and medieval England. Whereas tourism throve in the eighteenth century among the upper class, in the nineteenth it became far more widespread and more directly concerned with medieval survivals.[15] Thanks once again to the development and expansion of the railway system, which facilitated the inspection of the old as well as the new, tourism became a conventional form of leisure for those whose ancestors could not have afforded the Grand Tour on the Continent. Changes in language also mirror the growing popularity of tourism: Although the word "tour" was used as early as the seventeenth century, a new family of words including "tourist," "tourism," and "sightsee" all originated in the nineteenth.[16]

Another manifestation of the vogue of sightseeing is the enormous proliferation of guidebooks, individual volumes of

Tourists at the Tower of London, 1885. (By permission of The Illustrated London News *Picture Library.)*

which often passed through myriad editions. "It may be deemed almost superfluous," noted one writer in 1855, "to add another guide-book to those already existing for visitors to Hastings and St. Leonard's. Still the changes in public taste, the interest now taken in subjects formerly but little regarded" constituted sufficient justification to do just that, as did the lure of potential profits.[17] Travel literature was especially useful to the new class of the middle-class tourists, in search of historical and aesthetic erudition, because it offered them information on the histories of particular buildings as well as of cities and counties. It sharpened the sense of place and orientation of native and stranger alike by creating elementary visual maps that structured perceptions of entire landscapes as well as of their individual features, whether medieval or mod-

40

ern. Guidebooks highlighted the presence of the past both in cities renowned for their historical survivals, such as the ancient city of York, and in those more remarkable for their modern achievements and realities. The author of *The Historical Guide to Leeds* (1858), for example, anxious to bolster the image of the city by calling attention to its antiquities as well as its factories, pointed out that "even at the present time a break in the ground about six feet deep, the edge of which is paved and used as a footpath between Charles Street and High Street," indicated the location of the district's Roman camp.[18]

The pervasive taste for antiquities is also underlined by the fact that even groups avowedly dedicated to other concerns enthusiastically toured sites of historical interest. This phenomenon is exemplified by the British Association for the Advancement of Science, a largely middle-class organization, which held its annual meetings in such diverse locations as Cambridge and Manchester, Bath and Bradford, Sheffield and York, even venturing forth to the New World to take the gospel of progress to benighted colonials in Canada. Their travels reflect the development of a calendar of visitations for historically minded Victorians. It was *de rigueur* for them to see certain places, much as contemporary tourists dutifully "check off" various monuments as they "do" Paris or Rome. Whether or not the site of the annual meeting was known for its antiquities, the guidebooks prepared especially for these scientifically minded Victorians were replete with historical and archeological learning, even suggesting possible excursions and routes. The 1879 guide to Sheffield, for instance, remarked that if Sheffield had the reputation for being a "black town," such places as Conisbrugh Castle and Roche Abbey as well as the celebrated Sherwood Forest made the area rich in historical interest.[19] And the antiquarian Dr. John Doran wrote an interesting series of historical sketches in the *Athenaeum* in order to acquaint the British Association, as well as the general public, with the traditions of such ancient towns as Exeter, York, Norwich, and Bristol, which they were to visit.[20] Interesting as these guidebooks are, it is the records of the local historical and archeological societies that dotted England

The British Association visiting Bradford, 1873. (By permission of The Illustrated London News *Picture Library.)*

from Newcastle to Brighton, from Plymouth to Norwich, that furnish the richest evidence on the nature of the Victorian preoccupation with historic remains.

Their fascination with medieval antiquities manifests itself in the places they visited. One important group, the Yorkshire Archaeological and Topographical Society, made extensive sightseeing expeditions in which they visited such medieval buildings as Pontefract Castle, Kirkstall Abbey, Rievaulx Abbey, Mount Grace Priory, Byland Abbey, and Middleham Castle, to name but a few of the sites.[21] Not only particular medieval remains but entire cities renowned for their medieval architecture attracted these itinerant archeologists. On a trip to York in 1873, for example, they made a thorough survey of the Minster before turning to St. Mary's Abbey and the Guildhall. When they toured Wakefield in 1869, the party visited the "picturesque little village of Sandal" because it contained a fourteenth-century parish church, St. Helen's, as well as the scattered remains of Sandal's Castle, a fortress erected in 1317 by the Earl de Warenne.[22] Yet once again it is necessary to stress that compelled as they were by medieval survivals, Yorkshire archeologists, like their compatriots throughout the country, did not confine their attention to places, persons, and things medieval. During their visit to York, the archeologists dutifully investigated the city's remarkable Roman remains; and in their visit to Wakefield, they did not neglect the Heath Old Hall, a seventeenth-century building that one of their company praised as "one of the finest specimens in Yorkshire of an Elizabethan house."[23] The Victorian historical imagination ambitiously tried to encompass all ages of England's preindustrial past.

Victorian archeologists perceived antiquities both as works of art and as witnesses of history, as valuable for their historical associations as for their aesthetic qualities. Architecture became a lens for viewing history and history a magnifying glass for illuminating architecture. The investigation of historic survivals was meant to educate as well as to amuse: A speaker at the Yorkshire Archaeological and Topographical Society's visit to the Mount Grace Priory "hoped that when

people looked at the ruins and beautiful castles and abbeys their memories would carry them back to the days of those who lived in them, who were good men in their day, and to whom we owed the history of England, whether in the manufacture or the writing of it."[24] To ensure the realization of their didactic goals, the members of local societies and other eminent authorities delivered highly detailed papers on the places explored during sightseeing excursions.

Yet if the positivistic ardor for accuracy and information manifests itself throughout archeological literature, excursion reports demonstrate that there was a powerful romantic, imaginative element in the Victorian sense of the past. The vast expansion of historical knowledge did not blind Victorians to the "poetry of history." The *Wakefield Express* report of the visit of the Huddersfield Archaeological and Topographical Society to the ancient, venerable city is telling both because it reveals how one writer's historical imagination connected particular places with people and eras and because its purplish prose is typical of the rhetoric in which Victorians characteristically cast their responses to historic survivals.

> There are few towns in the West Riding, and we might even add in the broad county of York itself, that can boast so rich a store of important historical associations, or can present for the patient study and investigation of the archeologist so many objects of antiquarian interest as the good old Saxon town of Merry Wakefield. Foremost amongst its memorials of the past stands the grand old architectural pile, the Parish Church, calling up the pleasant reminiscences of Oliver Goldsmith and the "Vicar of Wakefield," and around whose time-worn walls are woven so many interesting traditions of the past; while nestling almost underneath the shadow of its noble spire lie the ancient seat of learning the old Grammar School, from beneath whose venerable roof have issued forth so many Wakefield worthies, being honored and distinguished names and the old Moot Hall,

with its musty rolls for six hundred years and relics of the feudal age. Equal in interest are the ancient bridge and wayside chapel, the former the scene of so many a bloody fray, and the latter much defaced by time, still one of the most elegant specimens of ornamental Gothic architecture to be found in the North of England... while but a short distance to the right and hid by trees, lies the scant and scattered ruins of that 'relic hoar of ancient days,' Old Sandal Castle, whose eventful history has formed the theme of many a poet's lay. These are some of the relics of the past that still remain, and around which our fancies play, weaving strange pictures of bygone days.[25]

Historical tourism broadened the imaginative universe of Victorians by affording them an ideal opportunity to play at being Saxon warriors, Norman conquerors, or Elizabethan merchants. Although the vision of "ruins in a landscape" dramatized the chasm between the medieval and the modern, these survivals also represented visible links between the past and the present. Thus, archeological investigations gave Victorians the illusion of historic continuity – an illusion profoundly appealing to those living in a world of exhilarating but bewildering changes.

The vogue of local archeology and history

Leo Tolstoy once remarked that historians answer questions no one asks. Many of his contemporaries would have disagreed with what might be seen as a prophetic remark. Thomas Macaulay's great *History of England* (1848–61) was a popular favorite, and Parisians filled the lecture halls of the Sorbonne to hear Jules Michelet hold forth on subjects ranging from Joan of Arc to the French Revolution. There was also good reason for Sharon Turner to comment in 1820 that "the taste for the history and remains of our great ancestors has revived and is rapidly increasing."[26] The study of medieval English

history from archival records did indeed make important strides during Victoria's reign, largely because of the editions of medieval documents compiled for the Rolls Series.[27] By 1866, with the appointment of William Stubbs to the Regius Professorship of Modern History at the University of Oxford and the establishment of a serious History School there, the professional study of history was well under way. Yet it is worth remembering that most of the greatest achievements in Victorian historiography were the work of self-taught amateurs, not professionals: Stubbs himself received no training in the mysteries of the archives, and Edward Freeman depended on his private income as he poured out the six volumes of *The Norman Conquest in England* (1869–74).

The nineteenth century deserves the title of "the century of history" because the passion for the past was not confined to major historians and their devoted readers. Indeed, one of the most remarkable aspects of Victorian culture was the vogue of historical and archeological activities, which were pursued by a wide range of English amateurs in their leisure. To determine who participated in these activities, what motivated them, and what aspects of the past concerned them, it is necessary to turn to the local societies that reflected and promoted the interest in history.

The rapid proliferation of these groups is persuasive evidence of the extensiveness of the Victorian fascination with the past. These societies were not, of course, without important predecessors: The work of such eminent organizations as the Society of Antiquaries of London (1717), the Society of Antiquaries of Scotland (1780), and the Society of Antiquaries in Newcastle upon Tyne (1813) come to mind; so too does the work of such distinguished individuals as William Camden and William Stukeley.[28] And the literary and philosophical societies that played so important a part in provincial intellectual life promoted historical as well as scientific research. But the point is not that Victorian archeological and historical societies were unprecedented, or even that they created radically new ideas about, and approaches to, the past. What concerns us is that they were collective efforts of amateurs; that they focused on

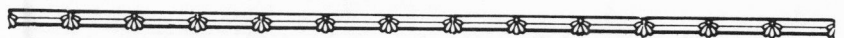

the local past; and that their very number highlights how fashionable historical pursuits were in Victorian England. The following list of the chronological development of these societies documents the booming interest in the local past in Victorian England.

1830s:
    Surtees Society (1834)

1840s:
    Berkshire Ashmolean Society (1840)
    Exeter Diocesan Architectural and
        Archaeological Society (1841)
    Yorkshire Architectural Society (1842)
    Chetham Society (1843)
    St. Albans' Architectural Society (1845)
    Cambrian Archaeological Association (1846)
    Sussex Archaeological Society (1846)
    Historic Society of Lancashire and
        Cheshire (1848)
    Suffolk Institute of Architectural and
        Natural History (1848)
    Somerset Archaeological and Natural
        History Society (1848)

1850s:
    Essex Archaeological Society (1852)
    Archaeological Society of North
        Oxfordshire (1852)
    Wiltshire Archaeological and Natural
        History Society (1853)
    Surrey Archaeological Society (1854)
    London and Middlesex Archaeological
        Society (1855)
    Bath Natural History and Antiquarian
        Field Club (1855)
    Kent Archaeological Society (1858)
    Leicestershire Archaeological Society
        (1858)

1860s:
   Huddersfield Archaeological and Topographical Society (1863)
   Cumberland and Westmoreland Antiquarian
   and Archaeological Society (1866)

1870s:
   Birmingham and Midland Institute:
   British Archaeological Section (1870)
   Croyden Natural History and Scientific
   Society (1870)
   Dorset Natural History and Antiquarian
   Field Club (1875)
   Shropshire Archaeological and Natural
   History Society (1877)
   Bradford Historical and Antiquarian
   Society (1878)
   Rochdale Literary and Scientific
   Society (1878)
   Bristol and Gloucestershire Archaeological
   Society (1878)
   Derbyshire Archaeological and Natural
   History Society (1878)
   Isle of Man Natural History and
   Antiquarian Society (1879)

1880s:
   Topographical Society of London (1880)
   Lancashire and Cheshire Antiquarian
   Society (1884)
   Lewisham Antiquarian Society (1885)
   Thoresby Society, Leeds (1889)

1890s:
   Southhampton Rambling Club (1891)
   East Riding Antiquarian Society (1893)
   Woolwich and District Antiquarian
   Society (1895)
   Hampstead Antiquarian and Historical
   Society (1897)

The names of these societies – "Architectural and Archaeological," "Archaeological and Natural History," and so forth –
are themselves telling, because they document the link between the concern with the local past and other popular Victorian interests, such as natural history and architecture.

This list demonstrates, above all, that historical and archeological activities were typical aspects of the mainstream of
Victorian cultural life: They flourished in London and in the
provinces, in urban/industrial and in rural/agricultural regions.
The bulk of the first local historical societies appeared in nonindustrial regions primarily for two reasons: Rural Anglican
strongholds were most deeply affected by the taste for medieval ecclesiastical architecture promoted so effectively by the
Camden Society; and mid-nineteenth-century England was
still mostly nonindustrial.[29] Yet it is not possible to make
broad generalizations on the relationship between industrialization and historical consciousness. The industrial city of
Manchester could boast of the Chetham Society (1843), whereas
Hardy's Dorset, an agricultural district, did not have a comparable institution until 1875. One possible explanation for this
cultural fact is that Manchester, like other provincial cities,
had a long-established Tory Anglican middle class as well as
an emergent Liberal Nonconformist middle class.[30] This said,
it must also be said that for the most part historical societies
were not formed in industrial regions until the latter part of
the nineteenth century: Huddersfield (later Yorkshire) Archaeological and Topographical Society (1870); the Lancashire and
Cheshire Antiquarian Society (1883); and the Thoresby Society of Leeds (1889). Until then those with historical interests
could pursue them privately or in a local literary and philosophical society. But whether they were formed early or late,
the existence of historical societies in the citadels of liberal
England demonstrates that the concern with the past was not
confined to marginal men critical of their own times.

Spotlighting historical and archeological societies in a predominantly industrial area, Yorkshire, and a predominantly
nonindustrial area, Sussex, provides a fuller picture of the
origins, composition, and functions of these Victorian institu-

tions that promoted the vogue of local history. The Sussex Archaeological Society originated, as we have seen, in response to the discovery of Norman remains in 1845. The founding fathers included the appropriately named Mark Antony Lower, who had come to identify the bones of William and Gundrada, not to bury them, and was a schoolmaster and the author of several works of local history, such as *The Chronicles of Pevensey* (1846); and W. H. Blaauw, a graduate of Eton and Christ Church, Oxford, both bastions of the genteel, the author of *The Baron's War* (1844). The first archeological societies in the heavily industrialized textile towns of Yorkshire's West Riding developed somewhat later in the century: The Huddersfield Archaeological and Topographical Society soon enlarged its scope to encompass the entire county's past, duly changing its name to the Yorkshire Archaeological and Topographical Society in 1870 and to the Yorkshire Archaeological Society in 1893; the Bradford Historical and Antiquarian Society (1878), by contrast, chose to concentrate on the history and topography of its own locality, making occasional forays into the regional past.[31]

The social character of Yorkshire and Sussex archeology defies ambitious generalizations. To paint a satisfactorily rich portrait of the individuals involved, one would have to know their occupations and residences, their social status and wealth, as well as how and when both were acquired, their religious and political beliefs and aspirations, and so forth. Most of this information is simply not available. Yet we do know that the leaders of Sussex archeology lavishly courted the landed classes for records they owned, the artifacts buried in their estates, and the prestige their participation would lend to the investigation of the local past. There was more, far more, than a trifle of snobbism in the Sussex Archaeological Society: Mark Antony Lower, himself the schoolmaster son of a schoolmaster father, gleefully reported to a friend that the society's July 1846 meeting at Pevensey was a "glorious success" because of the "presence of scores of Baronets, Colonels, Squires and Reverends."[32] He tried to ensure their continued interest by establishing a long list of vice-presidents in which the names of men who

were "honorables" by birth, if not necessarily by achievement, abounded. The majority of the members were aristocrats and gentlemen. Yet the rules of the Sussex society specifically prohibited political or religious controversy, and the membership was sufficiently varied to justify W. H. Blaauw's boast that the founding of the new organization was "met by the accession of 130 members of all classes of society, willing to cooperate in the study and elucidation of the history and antiquities of the county."[33] Not surprisingly, the composition of the Yorkshire Archaeological and Topographical Society reflected the social heterogeneity of the county itself, which contained industrial and agricultural areas, and an "old" as well as a "new" middle class. There, as in Sussex, the officers of the organization were often figureheads, eminent aristocrats, churchmen, and members of Parliament. Its real work was planned and executed, however, by a committee of serious amateur scholars, many of whom were Anglican or Nonconformist clergymen.[34]

The records of the Bradford Historical and Antiquarian Society furnish the fullest information on who participated in the study of the local past. Its membership list is especially striking for the social diversity it reveals. The best-represented groups in the society were businessmen, often wool merchants and manufacturers, followed by professionals, notably solicitors. Yet the organization also attracted many Bradfordians from the lower-middle class, including auctioneers and engineers, jewelers and lithographers, clerks and cashiers, as well as some working people such as weavers and spinners.[35] Why these different individuals joined the Bradford Historical and Antiquarian Society is unknown; but it seems likely that aside from genuine intellectual interest, which should not be underestimated, archeological and antiquarian pursuits were seen as paths to social respectability and advancement. This was, in all likelihood, especially appealing to those intent on bettering themselves, who could use meetings to mix with local notables. Although far more research remains to be done on the social composition of Victorian archeological societies, it seems likely that they were dominated by local elites.

The motives that led Yorkshire and Sussex archeologists to form their organizations and the purposes they expected them to serve are illuminated by their early statements of purpose. The fundamental aim of the Sussex Archaeological Society was, of course, to promote the taste for archeology "by means of the stimulus inherent in the communion of intelligent and well informed minds" so as to ensure that the county did not "lag behind in the present age of antiquarian research."[36] Historical investigations, like other cultural activities, were imbued, evidently, with the spirit of competition. W. H. Blaauw argued in 1848 that the "establishment of such a society may well seem to have been called for by the active spirit of the times, so willing to adopt things new, but yet so resolute to maintain the old, when worthy of its veneration."[37] Archeology provided a useful cultural compromise in that it allowed Victorians to devote themselves enthusiastically to the march of improvement but also maintain at least the fiction of historic continuity through immersion in the objects of the past. As Blaauw was also troubled by the decline in the opportunities for sociability in Sussex, he hoped that archeology, by virtue of its ability to "satisfy the requirements of the age," would help fill the vacuum.[38]

What motivated the founders of the Yorkshire societies to study the "early histories of their neighbourhoods"? Both the Yorkshire Archaeological and Topographical Society and the Bradford Historical and Antiquarian Society were formed by citizens who were disturbed by the dilapidation and disappearance of ancient monuments, eager to understand the great changes that had made their towns immensely wealthy and influential, and who believed that their new prestige demanded that the provincial past, too long neglected, be carefully examined. In 1865, at the first public meeting of the then Huddersfield Archaeological and Topographical Society, the group's president, Dr. William Turnbull, articulated one part of its rationale.

> Surely thus it is natural to ask what marks of such times are still to be found in our neighbourhood; and surely it is natural for the inquisitive mind to ponder

and reflect on the remarkable changes in everything...and to wish to know how, and by whom,
have these changes been brought about. It is well
known that there are many ancient charters and documents bearing on these points scattered among the
population, neglected and mouldering away. Our object, then, is to do something for the preservation of
these – to gather up whatever fragments can be found
– whatever will give us a glimpse of the customs and
manners, and employment of the earlier occupiers of
these lands...we wish to bring them, as it were,
into a focus, and make them useful to present and
future times.[39]

Exploring the past, then, was supposed to help Yorkshire residents orient themselves in a world of immense changes, which
had made theirs a region of great wealth and power but had
also impoverished its historical landscape. The collection, investigation, and preservation of antiquities was all the more
important because of the fear that the changes that had en-
riched Yorkshire materially had done little to elevate the minds
and uplift the taste of its citizenry. The connection between
the popular interest in local history and the growing concern
about the detrimental impact of materialism – a concern often
expressed by clergymen and professionals who were eager to
enlighten their self-made fellows – is revealed by a speech
delivered by the Reverend G. Lloyd in 1865.

Our age was becoming intensely commercial and we
find that the mind no less than the body required a
variety of food, when we run on month after month
and year after year in the same routine. When the
pursuit of wealth was almost the sole object of life
we are apt to take a low, narrow and selfish view of
our fellow men, and some of our noblest faculties
remain uncultivated, lay dormant and we know not
their value. Whatever therefore, turned our attention
occasionally into fresh channels, whatever would store
our minds with information regarding the past his-

tory of our race, whatever would add to our knowledge of man and his works, whatever as had been
beautifully said by one of our older writers, removed
our attention from the present and turned it upon
the past, the distant, or the future, tended to elevate
us in the scale of thinking beings.[40]

Historical and archeological study was but one of the many
cultural pursuits in which the polish of culture was applied to
the often raw world of industrial capitalism.

Yet if historical investigation was meant to be an antidote
to commercialism, it was by no means an antiprogressive or
reactionary force. It was, of course, retrospective, but it was
not necessarily an attempt to restore or idealize the past. "In
tracing out the customs and manners of our ancestors," wrote
one Sussex archeologist, "they saw how superior the present
race was to them in arts, in happiness and in prosperity . . . and it
was impossible for an archaeologist not to see that there never
was a time when England was so wealthy, so vigorous, and so
happy as in the present period."[41] In a similar vein, a Leeds
writer observed that the pursuit of archeology "enables us, by
a comparison of past ages with the present, to estimate properly the pleasures we enjoy, to love our country, to value
every privilege we possess, and infinitely to prefer the modern
period to any of anterior date, however glowing the description of it may be, either in the chronicled records of history, or
the . . . fabulous pages of romance."[42] These heady statements
suggest that if historical cultivation provided ammunition for
conservative intellectuals such as Carlyle, Pugin, and Ruskin,
for other Victorians it offered persuasive, and welcome, proof
that the belief in progress was well justified. The exploration
of the English past provided Victorians with a way to make
sense of change, to understand the dynamics of the "mighty
stream of civilization."[43]

Our Yorkshire and Sussex explorers navigated the "mighty
stream of civilization" in remarkably similar fashions. Their
programs were almost identical. In 1846, the Sussex Archaeological Society defined its purview in language comparable to

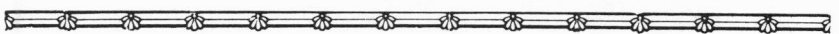

that later used by its Yorkshire counterparts, both of which consciously modeled themselves on established organizations.

> The objects of this Society embrace whatever relates to the Civil or Ecclesiastical History, Topography, Ancient Buildings or Works of Art, within the County...The Society will collect Manuscripts and Books, Drawings and Prints, Coins and Seals... Descriptive Notices and Plans of Churches, Castles, Mansions or other buildings of Antiquarian interest.[44]

They combined historical and archeological perspectives on the past, exploiting a broad range of literary documents and visual artifacts in order to obtain "some glimpses of the times in which they lived and thus be enabled to give a tolerably faithful representation of our remote ancestors."[45] To this end, historical societies made extensive excursions in order to acquaint themselves directly with old buildings, ruins, relics, and sites; undertook excavations to unearth buried survivals whose presence had been obscured by the passage of time and the construction of a new world; and published records series, in which they printed facsimiles of documents and objects, and journals, in which they reported the results of their researches.[46]

The contents of the Yorkshire and Sussex archeological journals reveal a striking similarity in the aspects of the past that attracted their historical imaginations. This is not to say, of course, that there was no variation from group to group or, for that matter, from individual to individual; but only to stress that Victorians in different sections of the country were fascinated by similar faces of the past. Proudly preoccupied as they were by the history and topography of their own localities, they rarely ventured beyond their self-set geographical limits. Aside from their provincial focus, what is most significant in their work is their visual approach to the past, their emphasis on fieldwork and their almost fanatical obsession with the historical significance of the individual object. Roman remains discovered in the Yorkshire moors, Tudor tradesmen's tokens found in Brighton, the last will and testament of a Norman bishop, the painted glass and memorials of a medieval parish

church, the worn fortifications of a ruined castle – these were but some of the artifacts in whose presence archeologists experienced what Johan Huizinga once called the "historical sensation."[47]

If their writings were, all too often, depressingly narrow – confirming Asa Briggs's quip that antiquarians tended to give equal value to every fact, even the dullest fact – their range of interests was impressively wide. It would be impossible to describe adequately the individual researches carried out by local historians in Yorkshire and Sussex, but it is possible to specify their favorite types of inquiry. They delighted particularly in describing the changing structure, iconography, and historical associations of local churches and cathedrals; the histories of domestic buildings, such as castles, the lives of their owners and residents, as well as the events that took place in and around them; the genealogies and heraldry both of notable families and of individual worthies; and the development of specific parishes, villages, towns, and regions.[48] Many of the works of Sussex and Yorkshire archeologists were concerned with the medieval past because Sussex was the scene of many crucial events in the struggle between the Saxons and the Normans and because Yorkshire contained some of the finest medieval architectural remains, both secular and sacred, in England.[49] Yet they venerated the Middle Ages more as a phase of local and national history than as a unique civilization. It was antiquity itself, not just one era, that preoccupied them. Indeed, the only period they neglected was their own: With the exception of a few interesting articles in *The Bradford Antiquary*, their own times were largely ignored. It was the preindustrial past, not the great changes of the present, that preoccupied local historians. Even in the age of progress, as the epigraph to this chapter suggests, the motto "the older the better" had its place. After all, nothing prevented even the most liberal-minded, future-oriented Victorians from looking backward as they moved forward.

Why the fascination with the English past flourished in both Yorkshire and Sussex is a question of basic importance. The

cultural convergence that we have observed is especially significant, because scholars have emphasized that the initial thrust of industrialization was to differentiate rather than to unify English communities.[50]

To understand why historical and archeological activities throve in industrial as well as nonindustrial regions, it is necessary to examine the contemporary concerns and realities that gave new meaning and relevance to the past. First, the social milieu and physical setting of both Yorkshire and Sussex underwent fundamental transformations during the nineteenth century, even though the rate and extent of change was not uniform. How to make sense of change was particularly problematic, because the social and material milieus of both areas had become complex mixtures of the old and the new, the past and the present, the medieval and the modern. Although Yorkshire's landscape was replete with textile factories and swamped with smoke, it also possessed some of the most distinguished medieval architectural survivals in all of England. And if Sussex was justifiably called the "holy Land of Castles and Abbeys,", it also had certain segments of the new technology.[51] Leeds, in brief, had the medieval ruins (Kirkstall Abbey) as well as industry; and Lewes had the railway as well as the monastic remains of St. Pancras. The exploration of the histories of artifacts, buildings, families, and communities helped individuals in both areas deal with the dominion of change by deepening their sense of place and orientation and fabricating a sense of historic continuity. Second, Victorians in both Yorkshire and Sussex needed strategies to cope with the consequences of the "birth of class" engendered by industrialization.[52] When the social structure of England was laid bare, the exposure of the conflicting interests, loyalties, and identities of different social groups intensified class polarization. It was precisely because of the depth of class consciousness and its potentially disastrous social consequences that it was important to find bases for communal harmony. Local archeological and historical societies performed valuable functions by furnishing opportunities for social meeting and intellectual interchange between individuals from different backgrounds. On

the one hand, they tended to mitigate social distinctions both between groups in the same region and between regions, through participation in, and acceptance of, common cultural attitudes, tastes, and activities. On the other hand, they may well have reinforced the hegemony of local elites, who assumed the roles of proprietors of the past as well as masters of the present. Local historical and archeological societies can be seen as institutions that, consciously or unconsciously, supported the dominant social order by facilitating social assimilation, by screening out problematic aspects of the past, such as socioeconomic inequalities, and by fostering the celebration of a common past. This brings us to the final, and by far the most important, cause of the convergence of the sense of the past in Yorkshire and Sussex. It was, above all, the strength of provincial pride and consciousness in both regions, and throughout England, that motivated and justified the exploration of the minutiae of history.

Provincialism and history

Provincialism is one of the most significant and least-studied aspects of nineteenth-century history.[53] It refers to the mentality of those who hardly looked beyond the confines of their own neighborhood, yet it also refers to the claim of the provinces, especially the industrial north, to be on a par with, if not superior to, London. If the long-term impact of industrialization was to centralize political and economic life and minimize local distinctions, its short-term impact was to differentiate communities, thus intensifying provincial consciousness and conflicts. Industrialization disrupted the balance of power, wealth, and influence by changing the relative status of different social groups and regions; it aggravated the struggle between landed and industrial elites, between and among old and new cities, and between the provinces and London. Rapid social changes made it problematic for classes and localities that had

experienced abrupt shifts in their status and affluence to cope with their new positions, for a class society infatuated with laissez-faire individualist ideals to find a foundation for communal bonds and loyalties, and for a modern civilization in which traditional social structures and values still persisted to determine what was respectable, prestigious, and admirable.

Historical and archeological explorations helped Victorians to deal with these problems because they furnished them with an invaluable source of provincial pride, identity, and consciousness. The founders of the Yorkshire Archaeological and Topographical Society believed that their county's newly won wealth and power demanded that its past be carefully excavated and publicized. Theirs was essentially a quest for what we would now call "roots." In his speech at the first public meeting of the group, Dr. William Turnbull argued that historical study was particularly rewarding in the West Riding because the alpine district, whose geographical isolation made it almost a kingdom unto itself, overflowed "with the memories and traditions and relics of the past." The investigation of the past was also valuable because the example of the dead, whether good or bad, could teach the living. One of the lessons was instruction in the origins of the character of modern Yorkshire people, who were celebrated, not least by themselves, for their pride, independence, and industry. As Dr. Turnbull put it, in a hardy, rugged language meant to appeal to northerners:

> There is also something attractive and something to win admiration; something noble and manly about the inhabitants of hilly regions. The fare may be simple, the manners unpolished; but the mountaineer has ever been found more hardy, more daring, more attached to freedom, and far more difficult to conquer than the dweller in the rich and sunny plain where flourish the myrtle and the vine. The sterile soil, the inclement sky, the difficulty in earning the daily bread...invigorate the nobler faculties and enable him to push aside and overcome whatever ob-

stacles in his path...Whate'er his lot in life...still
the mind ever reverts...to the haunts and scenes of
his youth.[54]

When the mirror of the past reflected such flattering images,
who could resist the urge to contemplate its reflections? One
Yorkshireman who could not was the Reverend Dr. Collyer,
whose move to New York did not prevent him from maintain-
ing a keen interest in the activities of the society. When he
assumed the chair at one of its meetings, he stressed that a
torn leaf from a parish register, a bit of carven oak, a rude
implement fashioned by the village blacksmith, a legend hid-
den away at the fireside, could all be restored again to "something like a warm and fluent life full of gracious meaning."
The task of studying and publishing material and literary records with a view toward eventually publishing a county history was crucial, because such a work would allow those in
"Greater Britain," which included America and Australia, whose
people were from Yorkshire to explore their origins. In so doing,
they would be united with their English brethren in devotion
to a common historical inheritance.[55] The exhumation of the
past, then, could strengthen provincial attachments.

The boom in the production of local histories in Victorian
England, like the proliferation of societies for the study of the
local past, reflected and revivified the strength of provincial
pride. Historian and antiquarian alike often happily assumed
the role of civic or regional booster: Mark Antony Lower, for
instance, dedicated his *Chronicles of Pevensey* (1846) to the
Freemen of Pevensey "with an earnest hope that their ancient
town, once so celebrated in the annals of England, may at no
distant day be restored to its pristine importance and prosperity."[56] One of the richest sources for understanding the relationship between provincialism and the sense of the past is
the *Historic Towns* series edited by Edward Freeman and William Hunt, whose first volume appeared in 1889. Mandell
Creighton's study, *Carlisle* (1889), is representative of the series in several respects. He examined the border city as a center of provincial life and stressed that no English city had a

more distinctive character or maintained it so continuously from antiquity to modernity. He frankly admitted that his work was the child of local pride, a sentiment he believed his fellow citizens shared. Fundamental to his historical vision was a concrete, almost sensual, love of the survivals of the past.

> Much as I have learned from books, I feel that I have learned more from many wanderings on foot through the Borderland. Its history is not to be gathered from records only, nor from the study of one particular place. Nowhere is the sentiment of the past so strong, not only in architectural monuments, but in the lives and characters of the people. It may be that being a native of Carlisle, my sense of local patriotism may have occasionally misled me; but I do not believe that my fellow townsmen, at all events, will be of that opinion.[57]

While Victorians were proudly congratulating themselves on the triumphant march of improvement, they were capitalizing not only on their manufactured goods but also on the survivals, traditions, and achievements of their respective local pasts in their quest for modern glory. Both old and new provincial cities participated in an informal cultural competition, which revolved around determining which community could display the most distinguished past, the prize being contemporary prestige and esteem.

To understand how Victorians perceived the histories of celebrated ancient cities, it is necessary to consider their perspectives on the present. Such writers as G. W. Kitchin, who contributed the volume *Winchester* (1890) to the *Historic Towns* series, were struck, and dismayed, by the contrast between their communities' medieval and early-modern fame and their relative modern obscurity. He modestly pleaded that his tale was necessarily one of the distant past because for centuries, indeed since the reign of Henry III, Winchester had struggled unsuccessfully with weakness and poverty, and had proved unequal to the position it once held among English cities.

61

Although he complained that Winchester was now hardly more than the size of an affluent Yorkshire village, he consoled himself and his local audience with the thought that in contrast to comparable medieval German cities, whose residents were content with dwelling on and in their ruins, Winchester had achieved a "modest prosperity and tranquility."[58] Reflecting on the rich relics of historic Carlisle, Mandell Creighton was impressed by the decline of the town in particular and the vicissitudes of human affairs in general. Yet he took pride in the fact that whereas by the mid-eighteenth century Carlisle had become a dispirited community, during Victoria's reign its population had doubled and it could justifiably be called "the neat and prosperous town of today."[59] Montagu Burrows, navy man turned Oxford professor, happily recorded in his work on *Cinque Ports* (1895) "not only past glories, but the singular rejuvenescence in our times of many portions of the ancient stock."[60] The stock of Exeter, a preindustrial industrial center of the staple trade, whose position had been eclipsed by the phenomenal rise of such northern industrial cities as Manchester and Leeds, had gone down considerably. Nevertheless, one guidebook writer proudly told how Exeter had become a "place of taste, elegance and opulence," and another compensated for the lack of modern industrial technology by boasting that local trade was pure – free, that is, from smoke and steam.[61] According to William Hunt, the citizens of Bristol, the great trading town that Liverpool overshadowed in the nineteenth century, had good reason for their "confident expectations that the commerce of their ancient city would continue to grow and flourish . . . and that it had a career before her not unworthy of her glorious past."[62] Although the perceptions and realities of the Victorian fate of eminent historic cities differed considerably, their boosters were united by the fear that modernity was passing them by, and by the hope that they could recover past glories.

These provincial cities compensated for the poverty of their industrial resources by highlighting the wealth of their historic heritages. The keynote was confidently struck in 1871 by the author of a Nottingham guidebook, who claimed that

few towns could boast of so high an antiquity.[63] Other civic boosters refused to accept his verdict. G. W. Kitchin claimed that Winchester was "the most historic of English cities" because its streets teemed with antiquities which recalled picturesque traditions and anecdotes.[64] "Among the most historic towns of England," commented E. L. Cutts in 1888, "Colchester had some claim to take rank as the earliest of them all."[65] The author of a guide to Hastings also proudly emphasized that its antiquity was "traced by various authorities to a very remote period" and that it was a "place of importance as far back as the Saxon Heptarchy."[66] "The earlier the better" was also the guiding premise of an Exeter guide who claimed that his city was a habitation "not only before London existed, but possibly before most other cities of the Island."[67] There is no need to transcribe comparable pretensions to antiquity made on behalf of other cities as well as for entire counties by their ardent boosters.[68] The claim to "high antiquity" was a cultural convention that reveals that "tradition" retained great prestige in the value system of Victorian England.

Recalling and publicizing the contribution of particular regions to the making of England also throve because it furnished communities with a rich source of identity, self-esteem, and national prestige. Although local historians were often notoriously unselective in their chronological recitation of event after event after event, the "one-damned-thing-after-another" technique did serve a contemporary purpose: to highlight whatever flattered a particular individual or place. Hence, importance was attached to comparatively minor occurrences, such as a king's visit, as well as to events of indisputably national significance, such as Alfred's compilation of a legal code in Wessex or the Battle of Hastings. Medieval history occupied a particularly prominent position because prestige seems to have increased in direct proportion to antiquity, but the antiquarian cum civic booster gladly appropriated past achievements and honors irrespective of their date.

The aspects of the local past that Victorian writers underlined reveal how they fabricated traditions that ratified their own values. It should come as no surprise that the commer-

cial achievements of the past, however slight, were seized upon throughout different forms of historical literature. This was particularly true, and appropriate, in a once-great commercial center like Exeter: "Exeter at a very early period," commented one writer, "became a place of considerable trade," a city in which a wide range of "mechanical business," notably the manufacture of wool, throve.[69] Underlining historic achievements tended to draw attention away from contemporary decline and disappointments. The genealogies of local self-government and of municipal organizations like the guild system also received special attention. Writers relished describing how and when their localities received their various charters and rights. G. W. Kitchin, for instance, demonstrated that Winchester "even before Alfred's day had a distinct civic life" and that it was a seat of government, administration, and learning by the age of Henry I.[70] Civic-minded historians also tried to assess the forces that had shaped the local identity. In *Bristol*, William Hunt set out to "explore some of the special characteristics of the inhabitants, the munificence and the public spirit of the merchant princes, the eagerness of its people to receive new things whether in religion or politics, and their independent and often lawless spirit."[71]

A final word on the social significance of the *Historic Towns* series: Although the individual volumes testify to the power of provincialism, their author's eagerness to stress the contribution of the locality to the nation and to show that its people were the most faithful representatives of "the English character" are also symptomatic of the nationalization of provincial cultures in the 1890s.[72]

Although provincial industrial cities faced dilemmas different from those of "historic towns," their representatives also found useful remedies in the past. Whereas historic cities' sense of inferiority came from their relative decline and their inability to participate fully in the march of improvement, the problems of industrial cities resulted partially from the abruptness of the changes their communities underwent. One Bradford

guide commented that the rise of the town had been so rapid that some feared that Bradford would never be permanent or stable.[73] The new industrial capitalist elite was in many respects enormously self-confident; but they too were plagued by a sense of inferiority, because their acquisition of economic, and to a lesser extent, political power did not win them the much-coveted badges of respectability. Anxious to reassert their hegemony in the face of the capitalist challenge, the aristocracy and their spokesmen branded businessmen as mere arrivistes, materialists obsessed with getting and spending, and unmindful of the common good. They were not, in short, gentlemen.[74] But businessmen were as likely to rebel against their image as to glorify the aristocracy. J. W. Turner articulated this viewpoint in a piece published in *The Bradford Antiquary* in 1888.

> That branch of literature which its professors are pleased to term history . . . decorates its pages with the sanguinary achievements of soldiers, or it sings the praises of pious, divine and learned lawyers, while the pioneers of the industrial arts and the collection and distribution of the nation's wealth are left to pass into oblivion unhonoured and unsung. The true fighting man from the unspeakable Turk to the British subaltern, together with his brother the talking man looks upon the workers and particularly the manufacturers and traders in the community as an inferior race.[75]

To mitigate the sense of rootlessness produced by abrupt expansion and the sense of inferiority fostered by the lack of respectable pedigrees, writers advertised the antiquity of industrial communities. "What would Leeds be with ten Town Halls and no Kirkstall Abbey?" asked a Leeds Radical whose history of his city hardly extended beyond the Middle Ages.[76] *The Historical Guide to Leeds* (1858) was entirely typical in its eagerness to demonstrate the presence of medieval architectural survivals in the centers of modernity: "We have picturesque remains of antiquity within a drive of us, viz., the

famed and time-honored Abbeys of Kirkstall, Bolton, Fountains, etc.; the castles of Pontefract, Knaresborough, Harewood and Skipton, imposing even in decay."[77] A similar tune was played by several Bradford writers, ever ready to compete with neighboring Leeds, who stressed that the center of the worsted trade was also the "centre and focus of a district peopled from time immemorial"; the "scene of many stirring episodes" of the English past, if now "quiet and industrious"; and, if not as rich in antiquities as some other Yorkshire towns, by no means as poor as some believed.[78] Not to be outdone, a Manchester guide claimed that the "shock city of the industrial revolution" had been "a place of repute from a very early period," a claim later substantiated by the scholars of the Manchester historical school, T. F. Tout and James Tait.[79] Perhaps the most striking example of the concerted search for the old in the strongholds of the new is found in Middlesbrough, a city whose phenomenal development had taken place almost entirely in the Victorian age. Nonetheless, R. L. Kirby, who was sufficiently courageous or mad to entitle a book *Ancient Middlesbrough* (1900), reminded his readers that the town was located on the site of a church consecrated by St. Cuthbert in the seventh century.

> The graver Muse of history would know that among those hills, and in the plain below, were the remains of castles, abbeys and manors whence had sprung... many a famous family of the Olden times. Middlesbrough may be absorbed in the Present, but it is not far away from a very interesting past.[80]

Just as Gladstone came to terms with the unprecedentedness of Middlesbrough through a reference to the Greek mythology so familiar to him and to his audience – he called it "our infant Hercules" – Kirby legitimized its modernity by accentuating its antiquity. The example of "ancient Middlesbrough" suggests that the myth of historic continuity was a psychological necessity for Victorians in pioneering communities, who were anxious to find sources of orientation and stability after the initial phase of expansion was complete.

The representatives of new as well as old cities advertised their achievements in the search for social respectability. Central to their vision of history was the story of the origins of modern political and economic liberalism. The authors of local histories and guidebooks highlighted the genealogies of local self-government and municipal institutions with an eye toward underlining the "overthrow of the old feudal power and the beginning of that civil and industrial freedom which is the flower and strength of a nation's progress."[81] Because the economic activities of the liberal middle class were far more suspect than their mainstream political ideals, it was particularly important to construct pedigrees for commercial and industrial occupations. "Romance sits at the door of commerce," commented one of the contributors to the guide for Bradford prepared for a meeting of the British Association, "sits with her distaff and wheels...but who will weave it into finished poetry?"[82]

This task was undertaken by many but was assigned in particular to John James, who was commissioned by the Committee of Worsted Manufacturers to write a history of their trade, and to Edward Collinson, who submitted a comparable sketch later published independently in 1854, as the lengthy preface to the Bradford Worsted Directory.[83] Both works were essays in the manufacture of tradition. Their basic thrust was to legitimize the textile branch of industrial capitalism, and to revivify the collective identity of its managers and workers, by demonstrating that far from being an upstart occupation, it was the "peculiar property of England," with a history as rich, romantic, and honorable, if not far more so, than that of the aristocracy. Both James and Collinson capitalized on the antiquity of the wool trade, tracing its origins to the classical Egyptians and Greeks, then following its course in the great medieval cities of Flanders and Italy before focusing on its development in England. Both argued that the rise of the wool trade was closely connected to the end of barbarism and the beginning of progress, and both stressed the great contribution made by its merchants and manufacturers to the prosperity of England, medieval and modern. And both saw history through

a commercial lens, evaluating institutions and individuals according to how their conduct affected commerce. How contemporary Victorian struggles and values were unabashedly projected back to the medieval past is illustrated by a passage in James's *History of the Worsted Manufacture in England* (1857):

> The reign of Edward III, ranks amongst the most glorious and prosperous in the annals of England. Before the close of his long and happy rule, the textile manufacturers and trade in general had reached, compared with the circumstances of the age, a mighty growth. Then commenced that rivalry between the aristocracy and the trading classes which has continued without interruption, to the present day. Before this period wealth was the possession of few; rank rarely attained except by military prowess; and slavery . . . the almost universal condition of the lower classes. Now the genius of trade enriched thousands; conferred the dignity of rank upon merchants and manufacturers; levelled the strong barriers of the aristocracy; broke the chains of the serf; spread the blessings of freedom and plenty, wealth and security over the land, and raised from their slavish and dependent state the commonality to the condition of free Englishmen, who by the innate energy . . . of their character, and steady perseverence, might amass fortunes for themselves, ennoble their children, and lay for future generations the foundations of their country's commerce and freedom.[84]

He condemned the medieval nobility for their incessant "interference" with trade as passionately as Richard Cobden and John Bright criticized the aristocracy in the days of the Anti–Corn Law League, celebrated Edward III for his sponsorship of "laissez-faire" ideals and practices, and applauded the guilds for protecting the rights of merchants and craftsmen but objected to their excessive "restrictions" on commerce. By picturing the medieval middle class as a heroic group bringing freedom and

prosperity to an oppressed, impoverished nation, James provided the modern middle class with a genealogy for their own values and with animating ideals to inspire them in the continuing struggle with the aristocracy. His work also illuminates another important face of the Victorians' sense of the past: Their vision of history was often anachronistic, because identifying the past with the present allowed them to preserve the myth of historic continuity and thus come to terms with radical social changes.

The historical, archeological, and travel literature analyzed here reveals that a concern with the past was an integral element of Victorian culture. The fascination with historic survivals, the eagerness to appropriate historic achievements, the pretensions to high antiquity, the penchant for ancestor hunting, not to mention the fine and useful art of ancestor manufacturing, were all cultural conventions in the age of improvement. The popularity of antiquarian pursuits undermines Matthew Arnold's oversimplified identification of Liberalism with a Jacobin hatred of the past.[85] English Liberals wanted to reform historic institutions and customs that upheld privilege and limited freedom, but this did not prevent them from appreciating other aspects of the local and national past or charting alternative traditions. The vogue of history also belies Lewis Mumford's idea that in the cities the "new masters of society scornfully turned their backs on the past and all the accumulations of history and addressed themselves to creating a future."[86] Although this generalization is wrong, at the same time it would be equally absurd to substitute the idea that the entire middle class was fascinated by the past. Certainly few businessmen wanted to run their companies like Ruskin's Guild of St. George any more than they would have been willing to don suits of armor and joust in the rain-soaked lists of the Eglinton Tournament in 1839. Few Victorians wanted to return to the past for more than a visit; but many found in their historic legacy a source of values and a sense of continuity that they used as signposts as they mapped out the road to the future.

Nationalism and history

"I suppose that no man of English race, and at all acquainted with the history of his country, can enter this city of York without feeling something of that respect of which all men are more or less conscious, and which, in the higher and nobler sorts, acts as an incentive to greatness in thought and deed."[87] This statement, which was made by a speaker at a Yorkshire Archaeological and Topographical Society excursion in 1873, reminds us that Victorians studied, celebrated, and ransacked their national as well as their local pasts. Major scholars such as Edward Freeman investigated both local and national life in their researches.[88] The civic-minded authors of the *Historic Towns* series stressed the interconnections between the development of their towns and the making of England. And just as archeological societies printed local records, the editors of the Rolls Series published national documents.

It should come as no surprise that the major elements of the Victorian vision of national and local history were strikingly alike. Both were dominated by the sense of change, continuity, anachronism, and progress. A few illustrations of this point from popular and scholarly sources must suffice. The contrast between the medieval and the modern worlds that struck our Wakefield writer also impressed the authors of national histories. Mrs. Markham, for example, in her amusing popular *History of England* (1863), noted that whereas medieval England was little more than an "overgrown forest," modern England was full of good bridges and useful roads and houses.[89] To compensate for the speed of change, Victorians avidly sought historic continuities in national and local life. Mandell Creighton qualifies as an expert witness on both counts, because he stressed continuity in his Romanes Lecture on *The English National Character* (1896) as well as in his *Carlisle*. "No nation," he proudly contended, "has carried its whole past so completely into its present. With us historical associations are not matters of rhetorical reference on great occasions; but they surround the Englishman in everything that he does, and affects his conception of rights and duties on which actual life is built."[90] The anachronistic standards by which John James judged the development of the worsted trade are trivial compared with Cyril Ransome's *Elementary History of England* (1890), a veritable monument of historical "present-mindedness." "I am led to think," he wrote, in a work intended for the use of schoolchildren, "that even the bloodiest of battles...is less attractive to the average schoolboy than the story, how, through the tenacity of his ancestors, he will have the privilege of keeping his own money in his pocket, unless it is voted for public purposes by his accredited representatives."[91] The Victorians coped with change through anachronistic devices and myths of historic continuity, both of which mitigated the contrast between themselves and their ancestors, and through ideas of progress that showed that change was for the best.

The Victorian cult of English history reflected and revivified national consciousness, pride, and identity. The idealization of King Alfred exemplifies how the national past informed the present. Long an English hero, Alfred was enormously popular with Victorians, who happily interpreted him in their own images and appropriated him for their own causes: for Thomas Hughes, Alfred's great achievement was the creation of a society based on mutual responsibility, a set of values that Hughes considered far superior to the cash-nexus of industrial capitalism; for Charles Kingsley, Alfred was most important as a hero of freedom.[92] Of the Victorian admirers of Alfred, Frederic Harrison has the greatest claim to our attention, because he was a leading figure in the English Positivist movement, one of the most radical and future-oriented of nineteenth-century philosophies. His idealization of Alfred is persuasive proof of the symbiotic aspect of the relationship between medievalism and modernity. Harrison believed that historical cultivation was an indispensable key to progress in that it revealed fundamental patterns of evolution and furnished contemporary culture heroes. He considered Alfred to be the greatest of Enlishmen, the herald of national civic and religious life, the

71

"incarnation of all that we must cherish in the national character."[93] He expressed this view in an address to the Birmingham and Midland Institute in 1897, in which he also suggested that the entire nation celebrate the millenary of King Alfred's death in 1901. Harrison believed that such a celebration would call for, and receive, the "representation of every side of our national life," because he was the only English worthy who "combined the honour of all."[94]

The millenary of King Alfred did indeed become the "festival of industry, art, order, union, peace and religion" that Harrison envisioned, and its story also underlines the powerful claims of local pride. Nowhere was Harrison's idea for a "permanent and visible" monument to King Alfred more enthusiastically seized upon than in the royal city of Winchester, which had been the capital of Alfred's realm. Alfred Bowker, who was the mayor of Winchester in 1897–8, when the planning of the millenary began, stressed that the townspeople had long felt the need for a memorial to their "greatest citizen" in order to impress upon every passerby that Alfred had spent much of his life there.[95] No less anxious to capitalize on the achievements of a historic hero in the search for contemporary glory was the lord mayor of London. He argued that London as well as Winchester deserved a statue of Alfred because "London is a great city and it was the work of Alfred...It was to London that Alfred looked for the starting point of that commerce which has grown to be alike the wonder and admiration of the world...It has been in London where the seed which he sowed of the principles of local self-government has found its home."[96] This interchange highlights the continued vitality of the rivalry between the provinces and London, a rivalry that may well have become more intense in the 1890s, as the increasing centralization of political and economic life made the provinces far less prominent than they had been earlier in the century.[97]

The millenary of King Alfred illustrates how the English used collective historic symbols to define national traditions. As Frederic Harrison had hoped, the planning and the execution of the millenary festivities brought together the representatives of labor, education, religion, and politics, because Alfred

was "all things to all men in the best sense of the word."[98] At the main events of the millenary – which took place in Winchester in 1901 shortly after the death of Queen Victoria – the speakers concentrated on different aspects of Alfred's contribution to England. They all stressed, however, that he was the embodiment of the national character and as such was a moral exemplar for all English people.[99] As the former Prime Minister Lord Rosebery put it: Alfred was the "ideal Englishman, the perfect sovereign, the pioneer of England's greatness. With his name, associate our metropolis, our fleet, our literature, our laws, our first foreign relations, our first efforts at education...the embodiment of our civilization."[100] Although Alfred was idealized as the archetype of the Anglo-Saxon race and as the founder of the Empire, there were relatively few blatant manifestations of racist imperialism at the millenary celebrations. Still, one event embodies the destructive face of nationalism: the launching in 1901 of the HMS *King Alfred*, a battleship equipped with all the latest armaments.[101]

The commemoration of the millenary of King Alfred's death became a "striking manifestation marked by every circumstance and ceremony that could impress the popular mind."[102] The visual orientation of the cult of the past manifests itself in the ways in which the patriotic aims of the millenary were realized. The main events of the festivities included a pilgrimage to sites in Winchester historically associated with Alfred, an exhibition of manuscripts and artifacts of his era in the British Museum, and a series of tableaux illustrating scenes from his life.[103] Noteworthy too is the commemoration medal. One of its sides contained an image of King Alfred with the inscription "Hero of our Race." The other side was decorated with a royal seal and an inscription that symbolized the historic continuity of England: "King Alfred the Great 1901 A.D. – Edward VII King and Empr. 1901." Also included was a testimonial to Alfred's relationship to Winchester and to local pride: "Alfred Bowker, Mayor of Winchester, 1901."[104] The greatest visual expression of symbol making was the immense statue designed by Hamo Thornycroft, which depicted Alfred in medieval dress, holding a sword in his outstretched arm.[105]

After the millenary was over, Alfred Bowker, then mayor of Winchester, wrote a valuable record of the proceedings and reflected on its contemporary functions. He believed that the historic celebration had stimulated the study of early English history, demonstrated English people's debt to their ancestors, revealed that the past was a rich source of moral exemplars, and shown the benefits of a moderate as opposed to an aggressive patriotism.[106] And he hoped that the celebrations, by drawing attention to Winchester's place in the early history of the nation, would one day make it the "pilgrimage place of the Anglo-Saxon race" – a prophecy partially fulfilled by the post–World War II tourist boom.[107] Proud civic booster he naturally was, but Bowker also emphasized the larger meaning of the millenary.

> The celebration proved an occasion when the most cultured of our race of all religions and sects, and of all shades of opinion, were enabled to meet on a common ground to do honour to a common ancestor. Such a meeting must quicken the feeling of brotherhood in the race, and should call to mind the great bonds of our common heritage, which ever firmly and indissolubly unite us in the eyes of all thinking people, thus tending to show if there be any gulf which is thought to separate sect from sect, or division from division, it is after all of the narrowest.[108]

Like the Reverend Dr. Collyer, who believed that a Yorkshire county history would teach those in "Greater Britain" whose families hailed from Yorkshire what their roots were, Alfred Bowker believed that the celebration of a common past revealed the fundamental unity of the English-speaking peoples.

The celebration of the millenary of King Alfred suggests that the appropriation of the national past mitigated the very real conflicts of interest, opinion, and belief that divided the English by furnishing overarching myths and symbols that were acceptable to most groups. The vision of a common English tradition helped transcend class, regional, ideological, and religious differences by strengthening collective conscious-

ness and attachments. It acted as an agency for cultural cohesion by screening out the disturbing social inequities that divided the English.

The fascination with history and its visual survivals was part and parcel of the improving, industrializing society of Victorian England. Victorians cultivated their historic inheritance for a variety of reasons: It provided a means to satisfy their desire for learning and self-improvement, strengthen their sense of provincial as well as national consciousness and pride, and confirm their belief in progress by showing that they were, for the most part, better off than their ancestors. Perhaps the most important reason the cult of the past flourished in the age of progress was psychological. Although many of the middle class were economically secure, the experience of rapid social mobility and of abrupt, profound change almost inevitably brought with it existential insecurity. Seen in this context, the sense of the past was particularly valuable as a source of orientation for those living an unprecedented life in an open-ended world. In any case, the study of history led to far less shocking results than the investigation of nature. It was one thing to discover that one's ancestors resembled Scott's Saxon fool Wamba and quite another to accept the idea of Darwin's ape adorning one's family tree.

Yet if historic survivals acquired new meaning in a world riven by change, their status in a rapidly expanding society was ambiguous. Their presence raised problematic questions, such as whether the heritage of the past was a burden as well as a boon and whether there was an intrinsic conflict between the pragmatic, utilitarian standards of a progressive civilization and loyalty to cultural symbols. To understand the Victorians' encounter with their historic inheritance it is, therefore, necessary to turn from their discovery of the past to how they treated its architectural remains.

3

The preservation of the past

> For like the Jews of old, most of us work with two
> hands; in one we bear a sword and fight for the works
> of our forefathers; and in the other we bear a trowel,
> and build up, as best we may, the works that are to
> express our age to future generations.
> —Heywood Sumner, "Protection and Production" (1895)

Improvement and conservation

Late in the afternoon of 8 June 1887, Frederic Harrison made
his way through the ever-expanding city of London to the
ancient borough of Holborn. That day his destination was not
the Positivist's Union, where he often articulated the tenets
of his creed as a layman; that day he would not lecture workers,
eager for self-improvement through knowledge, at a mechanics' institute; that day too he would forego a genteel, leisurely
tea at the Reform Club, where he sometimes discussed what
had happened of late at Whitehall and Westminster. Instead
he went to the Staple Inn, a distinguished seventeenth-century
building, best known today for its place in Charles Dickens's
The Mystery of Edwin Drood. There he was to address the
Society for the Protection of Ancient Buildings, an organization formed ten years before by William Morris and other
notables, who dedicated it to the proposition that modern
men had no right to tamper with ancient buildings, either in
the name of "progress" – which often meant little more than
the careless destruction of some of England's most beautiful
edifices – or in the name of "restoration," which translated
into a sophisticated form of vandalism. Surely Harrison could
expect to be well received, for he spoke with characteristic
flair and intelligence on a theme that all those present could
endorse unreservedly: "The Sacredness of Ancient Buildings."[1]

Frederic Harrison's passionate belief in the necessity of saving historic buildings indicates that historic preservation, like

archeology, was the counterpoint to, rather than the antithesis of, the Victorians' creation of a new world. The eminently modern barrister, who hailed from a family of architects, first acquired his "permanent zest for the history, antiquities and architecture of the Middle Ages" on a trip to Normandy he made at age fifteen.[2] As he matured, his youthful admiration developed into a more considered evaluation of the dilemmas raised by the presence of historic survivals in the midst of a modern society. Now as a committed progressive concerned with the problems of urban planning – he served on the London County Council (1889–93) – he knew that to "rail at the inevitable, to cry out for the past" was "idle, peevish and retrograde." Yet aware as he was of the necessity of change, the "awful, wanton and brutal destruction of the past" disturbed him deeply. In a series of essays on London, Paris, and other cities that he wrote in the late nineteenth century, Harrison described how the enormous changes he had witnessed had altered the visual appearance of cities, destroying all too many historic remains. The great question implicit in his works was how to reconcile the tension between the march of improvement and the conservation of historic survivals.[3]

Before turning to how and why Harrison and other Victorians tried to preserve ancient buildings, it is necessary to consider how the social pressures associated with industrialization shaped their fate. Urban renewal and reconstruction, as well as the expansion of the demand for new structures of unprecedented scale with the latest modern facilities, often rendered old buildings redundant. In 1897, for instance, the citizens of Peterborough decided that their town's prosperity and growth demanded the construction of a new town hall. Although some economy-minded individuals were uneasy about the large investment involved in such a venture, the real problem was what to do with the late-medieval guildhall that had served Peterborough for centuries but had become obsolete. Thackerey Turner, then secretary of the Society for the Protection of Ancient Buildings, implored the townspeople to save the "time-honored" structure, but some of the natives applied different standards to the situation. One man, who called him-

self "Civis," argued that the building was a "sad anachronism" in a "go-ahead" town like Peterborough. Picturesque it was, but there was no need to conserve it, as the town still possessed in the cathedral a building that "beat it in antiquity" – an extraordinary phrase which suggests that even this materialist was not totally blind to the lure of the past. Yet "Civis" maintained that in these severely practical times, utility had precedence over antiquity. Another citizen, not so modest as to forego signing his letter to the press "A Considerable Ratepayer," agreed, arguing that this useless "mediaeval doll's house" deserved no special consideration. It ought to be, and eventually was, razed.[4] This story reveals that Victorian philistinism was, alas, no mere chimera and that the desire for "improvement" sometimes did lead to the destruction of ancient buildings.

Yet this is only one part of a complex picture. The Victorians' veneration of the past did translate into efforts to secure its architectural remains, but they were bitterly divided on how this was best done. Certainly one privileged survival, especially for those whose taste had been formed by the writings of John Ruskin, was St. Mark's, Venice. In 1879, the Italian government announced a plan to "restore" the damaged West Basilica of the cathedral – that is, to bring the building back to an alleged state of architectural purity by sweeping away all historical accretions. This announcement outraged those who wanted to "preserve" St. Mark's – that is, to maintain rather than efface its historical character by authorizing only those repairs that would keep it safe, clean, and free from wind and rain. The campaign to preserve the cathedral soon won the support of many eminent Victorians, among them Gladstone and Disraeli, who found themselves in rare accord, both proclaiming that the plan to restore St. Mark's was an outrage upon history and tradition.[5] National and local newspapers took it upon themselves to spread the gospel of preservationism throughout the country. The *Daily News* expressed the main theme, arguing that restoration would destroy the "magical charm of the past, the sentiment that clings to every stone where every stone has its history."[6] Thanks to an effective propaganda machine, St. Mark's soon found de-

voted friends and passionate admirers in London and the provinces alike.

The compatibility of liberal values and historic preservation is dramatically substantiated by the fact that the first English public meeting to consider the destiny of one of the greatest monuments of the medieval Catholic past took place in Birmingham, surely the most radical and advanced of late-Victorian cities.[7] In November 1879, William Morris, who was the secretary of the committee to save St. Mark's, shared a podium with J. H. Chamberlain, a local architect who designed many of Birmingham's Neo-Gothic buildings. In his speech Chamberlain argued that although the English themselves had spoiled all too many historic buildings, they were at last learning their lesson. Thus, they had the right to call for the preservation of St. Mark's, as it belonged not to Venice but to the entire world. Another figure in the civic renaissance, the local writer Samuel Timmins, who was, significantly, the president of the Archaeological Section of the Birmingham and Midland Institute, also spoke at the meeting. He took as his text the proverb "Extremes Meet" in order to highlight the wonderful irony of such a "Conservative Meeting" taking place in "radical Birmingham." He proudly noted that the citizenry's concern for the destiny of St. Mark's proved that Birmingham was not, as some believed, a "town so practical that it had no taste for art." This comment is particularly telling because it suggests that on one level historic preservation was a way for provincials to show that they were civilized beings concerned with spiritual as well as material things. For Timmins, St. Mark's was "far more than a Church"; it was a place before which any thoughtful and sensitive person might stand and study the growth and progress of Venice.[8] By emphasizing that St. Mark's was a cultural rather than a religious symbol, Timmins made it acceptable to radical progressives concerned with spreading the civic, not the Roman Catholic, gospel.

These examples reveal that the treatment of ancient buildings was neither an abstract nor a peripheral concern in Victorian England. Confronted with the practical dilemma of what

to do with, or how to do without, a particular historic relic, Victorians had to determine what they wanted their world to look like, what ideals were the proper foundation for this world, and what price they were willing to pay to create it. In this respect, the treatment of historic survivals compelled Victorians to clarify their own cultural bearings.

From restoration to preservation

Although the restoration of medieval buildings was a favorite avocation of Georgian amateurs like Horace Walpole, it was not until the first years of Victoria's reign that this practice became a pervasive cultural activity. From the 1840s to the 1870s, Victorians enthusiastically restored churches, castles, country homes, and cathedrals. As architectural historians have made considerable headway in surveying these works, it is useful to examine the contemporary concerns that restoration expressed by focusing on the needs and aspirations of the clerics and architects who were its most avid promoters and practitioners.[9]

The relationship between religious revivalism and the vogue of architectural restoration is best illustrated by the Camden Society. This highly influential organization, founded by Cambridge undergraduates in 1839, was so solemn as to give seriousness a bad name. Dismayed by Anglican apathy, heterodoxy, and worldliness, these avid students of ecclesiastical Gothic architecture found in the Middle Ages a spiritual and aesthetic model that helped them reformulate the faith. The Ecclesiologists, as they called themselves, emphasized the role of art and emotion in religious experience, taking as their special province the "symbolical and material expression" of the Christian creed. Their fundamental premises were that only the restitution of the medieval stress on dignity, ritual, and sacrament could regenerate the Church of England and that this could take place only in authentic medieval settings. The problems they faced in translating these ideas into action were twofold: First, many medieval parish churches had been

shockingly neglected as Gothic fell into disrepute; second, the work of postmedieval architects, who ordinarily made additions to buildings in the style of their own era, often obscured, defaced, and eliminated medieval architectural features, just as the Reformation had wiped out medieval ecclesiastical practices. Architectural restoration was, therefore, an indispensable prelude to reconstructing the damaged fabric of the Christian faith.[10]

Thus, the Camden Society turned to restoration as a practical technique to transform the visual appearance of medieval churches in order to make them usable sacred symbols. "To restore," noted the first issue of their journal, *The Ecclesiologist*, "is to recover the original appearance which has been lost by decay, accident or ill-judged alteration."[11] Convinced that only they understood the true principles of medieval architectural construction and ornamentation, they directed the renovation of scores of English churches. How their ideals translated into action is exemplified by a restoration undertaken in 1841, which was intended to provide a model of their principles and a showpiece for their achievements. The object of their affection – I am tempted to say the victim – was the lovely Church of St. Sophia, Cambridge, one of the four remaining circular churches in England, originally consecrated in 1101. The basic aim of the work, which was executed by the talented architect Anthony Salvin, was to recover the "original design" of the church by censoring all postmedieval architectural features. Even though they knew little about the "original design," they had Salvin clear the pews and the gallery from the center of the church, replace the existing bell tower with a conical roof, and, in general, remake the church in the Perpendicular style they favored.[12] Not all restorations, of course, were as thoroughgoing as that of St. Sophia; but its treatment is typical in that it reveals how the ardor for religious purity on the one hand and for aesthetic homogeneity on the other led to the visual transformation of medieval survivals.

There were three main reasons why Victorian architects became exponents and practitioners of restoration. The first was, simply enough, that it was very much in their financial

interest to do so. Although there has been, to my knowledge, no systematic study of architects' fees, Peter Ferriday estimated that Victorians spent fifteen million pounds on restoration and, furthermore, that in the diocese of Peterborough alone, the "go-ahead" town of "Civis," £539,000 went into the restoration of ecclesiastical edifices.[13] The lucrative rewards obtained by restorers attracted a wide range of architects, from the most talented to the least competent. All too often they preferred radical surgery – the costlier the better – to simpler medicinal treatment. The second reason that architects turned to restoration was that renovating old buildings to suit contemporary functional requirements helped them meet the sudden expansion of demand for buildings, a demand that was a by-product of rapid industrialization. The final reason was that restoration provided a means for architects to define their own aesthetic orientation in a particularly problematic era. Industrialization created new building types and led to improvements in transportation that offered access to diverse building materials where only local materials had been available. Yet aesthetic possibilities opened up precisely when Georgian tastes and standards had been rejected resolutely. Thus, the burning question that preoccupied architects was, of course, what style was appropriate for an industrial, technological civilization. The quest for a new style was impeded, however, by the vast accumulation of architectural erudition. In 1858, the *Building News* argued that "our intimate acquaintance at the present day with examples of all styles has no small share in hindering us from working out one that will decidedly be our own."[14] Dominated by their aesthetic inheritance, uncertain whether progress was even possible in the arts, architects were often beset by a sense of belatedness and inferiority.

Seen in this context, architectural restoration was both a symptom of, and a remedy for, the Victorians' aesthetic limitations. The paradox is that architects created new buildings in the name of restoring old relics. In this respect architectural restorations were visual "misreadings," which varied in quality from the conservative or creative to the destructive or unimaginative. But good or bad, the flavor of restorations is

definitely Victorian.[15] Restoration is, therefore, a misleading name: What passed for, and was passed off as, restoration was in fact a species of visual transformation, a strange compound of archeological erudition with a cavalier attitude toward the past. It is ironic that the visual remains that shaped the sense of the past had often been restored so extensively that they were in some respects no less Victorian than medieval.

The full-scale revolt against restoration did not begin until the 1870s, although Ruskin had decried it from the first and even Scott had protested against incompetent, excessive work that departed from the "conservative principle."[16] The concern with the disappearance of the past was directly related to the cumulative destruction of countless historic buildings during the nineteenth century. The situation was well defined by the Liberal politician-historian James Bryce, one of the original members of the Society for the Protection of Ancient Buildings. In 1882 he argued:

> Whatever part of Europe one goes to – because it is true of almost every part of Europe – ... is the theatre of the process of pulling down the old and erecting the new in its place. The rapid development of the means of communication, the enormous increase of wealth ... and the mere ambition of persons to signalise themselves by great works, makes this the greatest building age the world has ever seen, greater perhaps than even the 12th and 13th centuries. The result is to extinguish everywhere the traces of the past. We seem as we drift down the stream of time, to go on with an ever accelerating movement, and to see the ancient features of the landscape amongst which our ancestors lived receding faster and faster.[17]

Although the fear of pastlessness was an important cause of the revolt against restoration, to understand why restoration was equated with destruction it is necessary to consider the shift in aesthetic sensibility. By the 1870s, the creative im-

pulse of the Gothic revivalists, who had directed and sanctioned restorations, was largely spent. More important, the ascendency of the Goths was undermined by their former followers, a new generation of artists such as Norman Shaw and J. J. Stevenson, the creators and partisans of the Queen Anne style. Mark Girouard has argued that historic preservation, like the Queen Anne style, was the product of a generation that appreciated the mellowness and texture of ancient buildings. Unlike restorers, whose aesthetic was based on stylistic homogeneity, the new generation valued historic buildings precisely because they combined the features of different architectural styles in an organic whole. Hence, architects like J. J. Stevenson found restoration insupportable because "purifying" ancient buildings deprived them of their "delicate charm."[18]

Thus, William Morris founded the Society for the Protection of Ancient Buildings (SPAB) in order to save the Victorian inheritance from further harm. The "duty of preserving jealously the very gifts that our forefathers left us, and not merely their sites and names" was a direct response to heightened awareness of the "destruction and falsification of our ancient monuments during the last 20 years."[19] The name of the new organization, which was soon nicknamed "Anti-Scrape" because of Morris's opposition to the restorers' practice of removing plaster from the walls of the buildings they repaired, is itself doubly suggestive: As a society it was the first major organization to concern itself only with the preservation of historic survivals; and, like archeological and historical societies, it was concerned with the fate of "ancient" remains in general, not solely with those of the Middle Ages. Indeed, it abandoned the dogmatic medievalism of the Gothic Revival in favor of a more relativistic, eclectic approach.

"What we require," said Sidney Colvin, Slade Professor of Art at Cambridge, "is a change of feeling...a revolution in public opinion."[20] The society's basic aim was to ensure that the historical and aesthetic integrity of ancient buildings were preserved by making only those repairs needed to prevent further decay and erosion. Just as present-day ecologists have tried to conserve the ravaged material environment, so too did

85

the preservers attempt to salvage the disappearing historical landscape. They promoted a transformation in tastes by propagating their ideas in newspapers and journals, having their politically powerful supporters lobby in Parliament for national legislation, and providing gratuitous advice on the techniques of conservation to the owners of historic buildings. In its first years alone, the SPAB became involved in controversies – for, as we will see, where the SPAB came in, controversy almost inevitably followed – over the destinies of the London City churches and Lincoln Guildhall, Ashton Hall, Lancashire, and Magdalen Bridge, Oxford, to cite but a few instances. Their work encompasssed Roman, Saxon, Norman, and Elizabethan survivals, pulling up short at recent history. Occasionally they extended their operations abroad, as in the cases of St. Mark's, Venice, and St. Sophia, Constantinople. Whereas our contemporaries are concerned with the preservation of entire historic milieus, the SPAB dealt only with individual buildings or with sets of buildings like the York City churches. This task proved formidable in itself.

Who joined the SPAB? William Morris, who served as the organization's first secretary, recruited many of the most distinguished men of the age, including John Ruskin and Leslie Stephen, Samuel Butler and Alfred Waterhouse, George Street and Thomas Hardy. The SPAB was, essentially, a London-based group drawn from an elite of the educated upper and middle classes, but it had numerous local representatives and supporters throughout the provinces. The diverse composition of the society reveals that the taste for historic preservation was not confined to the partisans of any one class, ideology, or faith. Nonetheless, it is significant that the organization enlisted the support of Liberals such as James Bryce, John Lubbock, A. J. Mundella, Charles Dilke, and Leonard Courtney. The driving force of this brilliant company, the committee that formulated its outlook and administered its policies, was dominated by William Morris and his friends Norman Shaw, Philip Webb, and J. J. Stevenson.

Before turning to how the preservation of historic buildings expressed their ideals, it is necessary to examine their critique

of restoration. In a now-famous letter to the *Athenaeum* published on 5 March 1877, William Morris outlined the basic charges of this indictment in response to the news that the Minister of Tewksbury was to be restored by George Gilbert Scott. His fundamental point was that the projected work would "falsify the Abby beyond recognition and therefore represented an unconscionable assault upon 'relics,' which scanty as they are now become, are still wonderful treasures."[21] Throughout the literature of the SPAB, restoration was consistently seen as "vandalism"; it "falsified" historic buildings according to modern conceptions of ancient designs and then rationalized this practice through exaggerated claims of expertise and empathy. Underlying this argument was the Ruskinian premise that modern workers could not recreate medieval architecture faithfully because they did not share the medieval craftsman's joy in labor. Their efforts, however well-intentioned, could result only in forgeries. Morris's other point was that the "destruction" of medieval buildings was largely the fault of their so-called friends: architects, who were "with few exceptions, hopeless, because interest, history and ignorance blind them," and clergy, who "are hopeless because their order, habit, and ignorance yet grosser, blind them." It was, therefore, imperative to protect ancient buildings, to ensure that they were treated not as "ecclesiastical toys" but instead were afforded the reverence they merited as "sacred monuments of the nation's growth and hope."[22]

The contradictions of restoration were humorously exposed in two cartoons that illustrate how quickly the ideals of "Anti-Scrape" were accepted by certain sections of the English public. The first appeared in the magazine *Fun* in July 1877, soon after the SPAB was formed. The opening frame depicts the Original Designer dressed in medieval costume, making a "simple and plain" column. Then we are transported through the centuries to a contemporary Victorian scene where we find a bedraggled and bemused cleric and a rotund Modern Architect with bulging pockets, standing in front of the column. The cleric suggests that the column, now little more than a ruin, is too small to restore properly. But this does not worry the

Modern Architect, who proudly replies: "Bless you, I've restored a whole cathedral from a chip of pavement." We might well believe him. In the third frame we see the new column, "something florid and complicated," clearly antithetical to the work of the Original Designer. Naturally the Modern Architect could not have known what the Original Designer had in mind; nevertheless he exclaims to the cleric that "all you have to do, you know, is to get yourself thoroughly involved with the *spirit* of the Original Designer." No sooner has this been said than the spirit of the Original Designer appears and inspects the column. He finds it alien and confusing and exclaims in frustration: "Well, what strange things these moderns do design. Quite unlike ours." And that is precisely the point.[23] *Punch* too had its fun with the restorers but did so more indirectly. Their cartoon is set in a "typical" Victorian middle-class home. Grandmamma has returned home one day thoroughly refurbished. When asked by her shocked children, and her even more shocked grandchildren, what she had done to herself, she calmly replied: "Well, my dears, all the fine old buildings are being 'restored' according to their original designs, why shouldn't old ladies have a chance as well?"[24] Yet try as she might, Grandmamma could not recreate her "original design," even with the aid of the latest techniques. Both of these cartoons cleverly reveal that the foundation of restoration was at least as shaky as those of the buildings intended for repair.

To understand how historic preservation served the contemporary concerns of late Victorians it is necessary to consider how "Anti-Scrape" perceived old buildings. Preservers, like archeologists, saw ancient survivals both as historical artifacts and as works of art. "The number of people who care for architecture is very large," commented one member of the society in 1878, "though as a matter of fact it is not the architecture they care about, but the associations connected with the buildings."[25] Frederic Harrison, for instance, argued in 1887 that ancient buildings were sacred because they were national creations whose charm and beauty were tied to the solemnity of the "genius loci." They were collective symbols.

> What buildings lose in personal interest they gain in
> human interest, in social significance, in historical
> value. The multiplicity of pasts in a great edifice, the
> vast range of its power over an infinite number of
> human souls, the concentration of efforts by which
> it was built up, and the countless generations of men
> who have contributed to its beauty, or have been
> touched by its majesty, give it a collective glory which
> no statue or picture ever had.[26]

Ancient buildings were vital institutions with continuous,
ongoing histories.

The realization that ancient buildings had futures as well as
pasts led "Anti-Scrape" to reflect on the contemporary functions historic preservation might serve. William Morris and
his SPAB disciples, such as C. R. Ashbee, W. R. Lethaby, and
Raymond Unwin, were deeply dismayed by the deformation of
English townscapes and landscapes and the commercialization
of values. The destruction of historic buildings, especially those
of the Middle Ages, deprived the eye and the spirit of a major
source of instruction and delight. Their preservation was a
visual necessity because their presence beautified an increasingly ugly, graceless world. It was a social necessity because
they were monuments of a civilization based on craftsmanship
and cooperation rather than mass production and competition;
as such, they symbolized an alternative style of life. Morris
hoped that historic preservation would revivify the aesthetic
instinct in ordinary people and provide aesthetic exemplars for
artists. For him, ancient buildings were symbols of the "triumphs
and tribulations" as well as of the continuity of art.[27] They
were particularly relevant to the artists, architects, and decora-
tors of the Queen Anne movement because their fabrics, which
embodied the life and art of succeeding generations, demonstrated the aesthetic possibilities of eclecticism. It was, therefore, imperative to preserve the art of the past in all its richness
in order to create the art of the future.

Historic preservation also revitalized the sense of tradition.
Because ancient buildings were, as James Bryce put it, "valu-

able records of national history and progress," their preservation revivified nationalism by providing symbols of Englishness. "The sense of historic continuity," Bryce contended in 1882, "is essential to the greatness of the nation as well as to the mental elevation of the individual. It even ennobles the details of our political and social life when we feel that we do not stand alone."[28] Ancient buildings had to be faithfully guarded, because as historic records that symbolized the continuity of English life they informed the national identity. The fear of pastlessness and the quest for continuity also preoccupied Thomas Hardy, who had himself participated in church restorations but looked back "in a contrite spirit" on his earlier work. In an address to the SPAB in 1904 he argued:

> Some may be of a different opinion, but I think the damage done to the sentiment of association by replacement, by the rupture of continuity, is mainly what makes the enormous loss this country has sustained from its seventy years of church restoration so tragic and deplorable. The protection of an ancient edifice against renewal in fresh materials is, in fact, even more of a social – I may say a humane – duty than an aesthetic one. It is the preservation of memories, history, fellowship, fraternity. Life, after all, is more than art, and that which appealed to us in the (maybe) clumsy outlines of some structure which had been looked at . . . by a dozen generations of ancestors outweighs the more subtle recognition, if any, of architectural qualities.[29]

The preservation of historic survivals provided a way to maintain and strengthen the sense of place, tradition, and community through the encounter with familiar objects in the material world.

Historic preservation is also significant when seen as a form of cultural orientation. It represented one way for late Victorians to define their own relative position, limitations, and aspirations. It was an attempt to formulate a viable relationship between the past and the present. "We cannot allow our

lives to be overburdened and crushed down by the mere accumulation of the dead things of the past . . ." argued the Liberal member of Parliament Leonard Courtney to the SPAB in 1878. "The real principle of our action is this: *"Let dead things go, let living things be kept."*[30] Vague as this pronouncement is, it nonetheless suggests that the members of the SPAB were intent on preserving only those aspects of the past that still possessed contemporary value and significance. Their attitude toward historic survivals was based on the recognition that it was impossible to faithfully restore or recreate ancient architecture. This realization had important implications. It meant that moderns had no right to tamper with ancient buildings. Their trust was to preserve them because, as Frederic Harrison put it, they were part of "the inheritance which the past is bequeathing to the future and of which we are but trustees."[31] The implication of Norman Shaw's idea that "servile imitation" of the art of the past resulted only in "lifeless copies" was that moderns had to create new forms of aesthetic expression.[32] The SPAB's cultural compromise was to balance the sword with which they fought for the works of their forefathers and the trowel with which they built a new art.

What is finally most remarkable about historic preservation is that it was future oriented. It was concerned with the functions historic buildings could serve in the present and for posterity, and it was connected with the search for new forms of aesthetic expression. Historic preservation appealed to many utopians and conservatives alike because it ensured the presence of the landmarks of the past in the nowhere land of the future.

That is why it was perfectly appropriate for Frederic Harrison to be the keynote speaker of the SPAB's annual meeting in 1887. Before he delivered his able address, William Morris saw fit to introduce his guest with a few comments on the theme he had selected to speak on. Morris was glad that his compatriot had used the word "sacred" to describe ancient buildings, for he too believed that there is "something wider and deeper than the mere utilitarian feeling about matters of this sort, that there is what you may honestly and formlessly call a

religious feeling that all parties and creeds may entertain."[33] The representatives of one creed, or, more precisely, of one organization, evidently agreed: As the meeting was about to adjourn, Mr. Hughes of the Prudential Assurance Company, the owners of the Staple Inn, proudly announced that the management had decided to preserve the building on account of its historic value. This, he maintained, should do something to dispel the widespread notion that "commercial companies have no sentiment."[34]

The 1887 meeting poses significant questions. To determine to what extent the ideal of historic preservation was a religious feeling that all creeds entertained and to discover what happened when owners of ancient buildings proved less generous than the Prudential Assurance Company, we must move beyond London and the elite world of the Staple Inn. Through detailed case studies of the late-Victorian fates of particular medieval buildings, it is possible to illuminate the contemporary concerns historic preservation expressed and how social, economic, political, and religious interests shaped the treatment of historic survivals. The examples that follow were chosen for purposes of contrast: One took place in an industrial city; the other, in a historic town. One concerned a building in ruins; the other, buildings in use. Although the campaigns to save the buildings in question were both successful, these cases are not presented here as evidence, much less conclusive proof, that efforts at preservation were successful more often than not. The story of the demolition of the Peterborough Town Hall is but one illustration of the Victorians' destruction of the survivals of the past. The interest of the cases examined here rests not in their happy endings — which might easily have been different — but in what they reveal about Victorian attitudes toward the medieval legacy.

Kirkstall Abbey, Leeds

"The ruins . . . are seated on the banks of the Aire amidst picturesque sylvan scenery, while although so near to the busy man-

Kirkstall Abbey, circa mid-nineteenth century. (By permission of the National Monuments Record.)

ufacturing town where the struggle for daily existence is so earnest and labourious, yet the charm of seclusion peculiar to monastic ruins, is perfect."[35] The remains in question were those of Kirkstall Abbey, a Cistercian monastery founded in 1152 near what later became the industrial city of Leeds. By the late nineteenth century, when our story begins, the Cistercians had long departed, leaving behind them the bare ruined choirs of a monastery by then enveloped in a "perpetual pall of smoke," which came from nearby factories. Over the centuries Kirkstall Abbey had slowly disintegrated: It was unroofed at the Suppression, part of its tower collapsed in 1792, and by the 1880s its vaulting and walls were extremely fragile. Yet even in fragments, Kirkstall Abbey, more than any other building of its type, remained the same in its arrangements as on the date of its erection.[36]

To understand how the people of Leeds and its region responded to the threats to Kirkstall Abbey, it is necessary to consider how it contributed to the sense of place. It is difficult to determine precisely how it fit into their image of the city because historians, unlike students of contemporary cities,

Leedsers at Kirkstall Abbey, circa mid-nineteenth century. (By permission of the National Monuments Record.)

cannot question their subjects directly.[37] Yet we do know that Kirkstall Abbey was a unique feature in the visual map of Leedsers for several reasons. It was, first of all, a junction: Located on the outskirts of the city, it was ten minutes by foot from both the Northeastern and the Midlands railways and five minutes from the trams. It gave its name to the industrial district that surrounded it. It was an especially useful, memorable landmark because its medieval architecture contrasted dramatically with the predominantly Victorian townscape of Leeds.

Kirkstall Abbey occupied a unique place in people's imaginative as well as visual maps. It was the subject of poems, histories, and paintings, the site of archeological excavations, as well as a major attraction for tourists. As the chief medieval relic in the borough of Leeds, it attracted the attention of the Yorkshire Archaeological and Topographical Society and the Bradford Historical and Antiquarian Society, both of which organized excursions to it. Memory, habit, and association all conspired to transform this open space into a privileged place. Yet like any other place, Kirkstall Abbey was by no means experienced in the same way by everyone. It had different meanings for lovers who used it for secret meetings and for antiquarians who studied it for learned papers; for children who grew up in its prospect and for travelers who saw it briefly on a hurried visit.

If there was no single vision of Kirkstall Abbey, Victorians did perceive the ruins through the lens of the picturesque aesthetic. The romantic appeal of the remains was ably evoked by J.M.W. Turner's friend Thomas Girtin in his painting *Kirkstall Abbey – Evening* (circa 1800). What is most important in this tranquil scene is the almost complete identification of architecture and nature. The artist emphasized the harmonious relationship of the abbey to its surroundings by barely differentiating the ruins from the trees that envelop it and by placing it in the background rather than the foreground of the painting so that it blends into rather than dominates the scene. The ruins also furnished a scenic backdrop for a poem by a local man, the Reverend David McNicholl's "An Elegy upon the Ruins of Kirkstall Abbey" (1836), in which he rapturously recorded his delight in the "soft pleasures of this wilder'd scene."[38] Even in the 1880s the conventions of the picturesque still structured Victorian responses to the medieval ruins and how they were expressed. Consider the language and imagery, for instance, of a Whitsuntide poem of 1883, written by another Leeds poet, George Hill. He was especially struck by the contrast between the abbey's medieval and modern conditions:

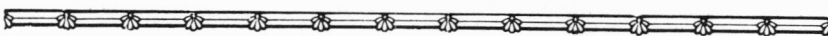

> 'Mid roofless aisle and broken arch,
> Kirkstall! I wander, musing o'er
> Thy ancient glory, and the march
> Of the long ages which have sped
> Since first thy lofty pile was reared
> By Aire's lone bank, when the first
> Plantagenet ruled in England.
> Old time has left its mark upon thee,
> Strewing floor and greenward all around
> With thy rich spoils – capital and shaft,
> Corbel and mullion – all in rude
> Confusion lie, the wreck of bygone
> Ages!

Disturbed as he was by the destruction of the abbey, Hill ended his poem on a conventionally optimistic note, finding consolation for evanescence in the perpetual renewal of nature.

> ...fresh verdure
> Crowns the trees, and songs of tuneful
> Birds conspire to charm; the sunlight
> Gilds the walls, new life and joy are
> here –
> Forget the shadowy past! Let all be glad.[39]

Yet as we will see, many of the townspeople did not want to forget the shadowy past, although they also refused to let its penumbra obscure the light of the present.

Victorians responded to Kirkstall Abbey as an artifact of history as well as a work of nature. The story of its foundation was narrated in detail – if in detail interpreted more in the spirit of romance than in the spirit of accuracy – by yet another Leeds poet, Dr. John Ryley Robinson. His "Kirkstall Abbey" (1885) is most interesting because it stressed that the abbey was a survival of the medieval Catholic past. He had little sympathy for the age he described.

> ...lovely damsels at confessionals
> Breathing their secret hopes into the ears
> Of young, unmarried licentious monks.[40]

Robinson was no more loath to point out that the abbots had derived substantial material gain from the deathbed recoveries of those they tended than he had been to highlight the unsatisfied desires of the monks. He concluded his historical tale, in true Victorian fashion, with a timeless lesson: Those who live a blameless, holy life on earth will enjoy eternal salvation. That medieval Catholicism, like the abbey itself, was in ruins did not disturb him. Nor did it disturb an earlier writer whose admiration of Kirkstall Abbey did not conflict with the belief that the nineteenth century was an age of progress:

> Since the day when Henry de Lacy brought the Cistercians to this sweet retreat how changed are the scenes which the River looks upon! Then...the deer, wild boar and white bull were wandering in unfrequented woods, or wading in untainted waters, or roaming over boundless heaths. Now hundreds of thousands of men, of many races have extirpated the wood, dyed the waters, with tents derived from other lands, turned the heath into textile fields and filled the valleys with mills and looms...Yet not all the beauty of Airedale is lost; nor should the thoughtful mind which now regards the busy stream of the Aire, lament the change. The quiet spinner is happier than the rude and violent hunter; the spirit of true religion fills these populous villages, as well as it once filled those cloistered walls. The woods are gone, and in their place the iron road; but that road conducts the intelligent lover of beauty to other hills and dales where art has no contest with nature, and by enabling him to compare one region with another, corrects his judgement, heightens his enjoyment, and deepens his sympathy with man.[41]

Kirkstall Abbey was also an aesthetic exemplar and a cultural symbol. In "A Lecture for the People" delivered at the Leeds Architectural Association in 1886, the local architect James W. Connon reconstructed the style of life and art of the

monastery in a fashion that would have satisfied archeologists. He admired particularly the simplicity and directness of the architecture, likening the Cistercians, significantly, to the Quakers in that both groups scorned the pomp and display of other religious bodies. We can presume that this opinion was shared by many others in Leeds, well represented as it was with Nonconformists, who might have had some difficulty in accepting the richly ornamented iconography of other medieval Catholic art forms. If Kirkstall was representative of medieval ecclesiastical architecture, Connon commented, contemporaries ought to refrain from "feeling proud of our modern efforts; even where we do try to build a church worthy of its uses; our greatest efforts are put to shame." Although Victorians had little doubt that they were in most respects superior to their ancestors, their assurance did not extend to the quality of their works of art. Connon concentrated in his lecture on the architectural history of Kirkstall Abbey, but he also stressed that it was valuable as a historical record. The strategy he employed to screen out the Catholic associations of the abbey was to present it to his audience as an embodiment of the "silent records of the labours, the endurance, the steadfastness of those who paved the way for their country's greatness."[42] Victorians needed to remake the past in their own image to feel comfortable with its survivals.

Given the privileged status of Kirkstall Abbey, the question of its future was not a trivial consideration. One vision of the Cistercian ruins' potential functions was put forth by Colonel Edward Akroyd, a wool magnate from the neighboring industrial town of Halifax, one of the new masters of English society who was very much aware of the value of the nation's historic and aesthetic inheritance. He hoped to restore Kirkstall Abbey so that it could serve as a church once more. Thus, Akroyd and a committee of Leeds gentlemen commissioned the unfortunately indefatigable George Gilbert Scott to inquire into the "cost and practicability" of bringing Kirkstall Abbey back to a state fitted to its sacred uses.

Scott's report on the restoration of Kirkstall Abbey is significant in several ways. First, he argued that all its buildings – of

whose artistic quality he found it "impossible to speak too highly" – were certainly the product of one mind and the work of one age. This claim justified his plan to restore the abbey to its homogeneous "original design." Second, the basic aesthetic goal of the work he projected was to ensure that all could see that "Kirkstall Abbey has been a *ruin* and has been rescued." This curious compromise between the claims of the present and the past manifests itself throughout his plan. He resolved, for instance, to make the interior of the church "seemly" once again, but chose not to obliterate the corrosions and stains that "three hundred winters had made upon the interior." He wanted them to remain in commemoration, however humiliating, of those long centuries of neglect. Surely when the work was complete the church would be as good as new, but perhaps not as good as old. Third, to Scott's eyes even the charm and poetry of the ruins were tainted by the fact that its picturesque effects were the outcome of ruthless desecration and neglect. Although he admitted, rather hesitantly, that restoring the medieval church might result in the loss of some of its picturesque quality, he argued that the "clashing with antiquity by the reconstruction of the building would be but small." Not so the cost! He estimated that the restoration of this "noble and sacred" edifice would amount to £34,250, not an inconsiderable sum even to Akroyd and his prosperous fellows.[43] We do not know whether they believed the cost was exorbitant or the benefits limited but, at all events, the plan was never put into action.

James Connon's lecture on Kirkstall Abbey reveals that by 1886 certain circles in Leeds as well as in London had rejected the restorers' approach to historic buildings. He called Scott's plan absurd and commented that he was sure that no one in the audience would have assented to a scheme that would have robbed the ruins of all their interest. For him, as for "Anti-Scrape," whose influence is manifest both in his ideals and his rhetoric, restoration was desecration. Although he believed that the people of Victorian Leeds were far more aware of the aesthetic and historic value of Kirkstall Abbey than their ancestors had been, nonetheless they had done lit-

tle to conserve it. This he construed as yet another sad symptom that in these matters the "idle male Briton is always prone to mischief and careless demolition." The existence of so notable a work of art in their midst laid a duty upon all those who valued beauty, all who cared for the records of their nation's art, to come to the rescue of Kirkstall's time-worn walls.[44]

The options open to late Victorians concerned with historic preservation were radically limited by the absence of governmental controls. Despite the efforts of leading Liberals such as John Lubbock, James Bryce, Charles Dilke, and Leonard Courtney – all of whom were members of the SPAB – not until 1913 was there parliamentary legislation that effectively controlled the treatment of old buildings. The major reason for opposition to measures calling for protection of ancient monuments was the strength of private-property rights.[45] The fear that an Englishman's home would no longer be his castle was no idle threat at Westminster, where more than a few members actually lived in castles and more than a few others aspired to do so. The only viable alternatives for those like James Connon who wanted to secure particular historic survivals was to act independently or turn to the SPAB for help. Laissez-faire was, therefore, the order of the day, but the case of Kirkstall Abbey reveals what a confusing order it was.

The campaign to save the Cistercian ruins began in September 1882, when two citizens of Leeds wrote independently to the SPAB to enlist the organization's aid in saving the abbey, which they feared was "crumbling fast" and would soon be beyond repair.[46] Kirkstall Abbey was part of the vast estate of the late Lord Cardigan, the mad hero of Crimea, whose family had owned it since 1671; it was now managed by an agent, B.E. Bennett, on behalf of Lady Cardigan, the earl's widow. One of the SPAB's local representatives, W. C. Marshall, ascertained that the "Cardigan family do not appear to take any interest in their property here except as a source of income."[47] Thus, Bennett had rented Kirkstall Abbey to a local man, John Octavius Butler, but he did not have the resources to repair it.

101

The SPAB decided to take on the case, and so in October 1882 its secretary, Thackeray Turner, wrote the first of what would be a series of letters to agent Bennett in which he informed him that the condition of the abbey was a "matter of great interest to those in the neighbourhood."[48] But this did not interest Bennett, who proved his indifference by ignoring the correspondence. Having failed with him, the SPAB turned to local allies, such as Edmund Wilson, a leading local Liberal councillor who was also a prominent member of the Yorkshire Archaeological and Topographical Society.[49] From October 1882 to June 1883, Wilson did his best to secure Kirkstall Abbey, first by attempting to purchase it, then by trying to lease it. After numerous delays Bennett refused his offer but offered, in turn, to let concerned Leeds gentlemen pay for the necessary repairs. Bennett's excuse for his refusal was the "great pride in holding the Abbey as part of the Cardigan Estate"; but it is far more likely that being shrewd, if not generous, he recognized that the market value of the property was greater than he supposed and resolved to capitalize on it. There is also evidence that he was annoyed by the insistent interference of "Anti-Scrape" in his affairs. Marshall, fearing precisely that, had tried to convince Turner and his fellows to "tread lightly." This, he admitted, was a "Leedser's point of view," but the "brass will have to come out of the Leedser's breeches pockets."[50] Yet for the present the plan had failed. By the time action resumed in 1888, Turner, for one, recognized that it was necessary to acquire the ruins and grounds as public property and then make the repairs as need be.[51]

The fate of Kirkstall Abbey seemed more precarious than ever before when, in the summer of 1888, representatives of the Cardigan Estate advertised its public sale. "Important freehold historical estates," the notice began, "embracing the Ancient Ruins of Kirkstall Abbey, unequalled in magnificence, and said to be the most interesting and perfect specimen of any Monastic Edifice in the country, presenting a gem of rich Architectural Beauty," could now be purchased.[52] When this extraordinary advertisement first appeared, people in Leeds and other towns expressed their astonishment and suggested

several ways to prevent the abbey from falling into the wrong hands. The *Birmingham Daily Post* pointed to the gravity of the situation as evidence that England needed some reliable means of protecting historic buildings. Although it was hoped that the SPAB would make an effort to save the abbey, it was ultimately the responsibility of the nation to protect it from the "unscrupulous speculator" and the ignorant restorer.[53] The *Leeds Mercury*, the town's liberal newspaper, agreed that Kirkstall must be protected from the "caprice of any chance purchaser and from the ravages of time."[54] In a forceful editorial it called upon the town council to take speedy action. "The question," it stressed, "is preeminently one for the careful consideration of the Corporation."[55] Not all the townspeople, however, were convinced that this way of making the abbey part of the "fabric of the community" would be effective, and therefore they put forth other ideas. Given the fact that Leeds was already heavily rated, one suggestion was to take up a subscription fund, to which each could donate what could be afforded, with the prosperous carrying the bulk of the burden.[56] Finally, one man suggested that a wealthy citizen, anxious to perform a great public service, might buy the abbey for the benefit of all.[57]

Several of these options were pursued simultaneously. A group of Leeds gentlemen formed a committee to negotiate for the purchase of the abbey, because they feared that the town council might prove indecisive in this affair. Their plan was to have the committee purchase the abbey with its own funds and donate it to the townspeople for their "use and enjoyment," with the expectation that they would be reimbursed by the Leeds Corporation in the near future.[58] They did indeed move quickly, making an offer to Lady Cardigan in mid-September, but unfortunately she refused their bid. Meanwhile, the Leeds Corporation, responding to public pressure, did begin to consider the matter. Although the council finally adopted Edmund Wilson's motion calling for the corporation to purchase Kirkstall Abbey, so too did they adopt a wait-and-see attitude, deciding to watch the progress of the negotiations carefully so that they might step in at the most propitious

moment, salvaging the abbey at the lowest cost to the public. The desire for economy shaped their strategy.

The Cardigan Estate, intent upon obtaining the highest price possible, decided to auction off what Lady Cardigan fondly called the "ruins of her grand old Abbey." At the auction, which took place in the late autumn of 1888, the designated representative of the Leeds Corporation, Sir George Morrison, bid five thousand pounds for the abbey only to find his bid countered by his competition. The auctioneer finally announced that as the reserve was ten thousand pounds, he would accept nothing less. As the proceedings ended, he commented harshly that the Leeds Corporation "should be a little bit quicker and adapt themselves to the times."[59] The notion of progress, evidently, had many peculiar uses. Clearly dissatisfied with the results of the auction, the Cardigan Estate decided to make the property more attractive by dropping the stipulation that prospective buyers had to agree that no new buildings would be erected on the grounds. This move encouraged speculators who preferred a free hand in developing this unique piece of real estate, and soon the Cardigan Estate had the offers they had hoped for.

It was at this point that Edmund Wilson, with the aid of a few friends, made a provisional contract with the trustees of the Cardigan Estate for the purchase of Kirkstall Abbey. The *Times* reported that he did so after it was ascertained that a promoter of public entertainments was trying to buy the ruins.[60] Wilson set about looking for other well-to-do citizens who might help defray the cost of his civic-minded action. When aid did come, it was both accidental and unexpected. Around the same time that Wilson purchased the abbey, two representatives of the Leeds Mechanics' Institute paid a visit to Colonel John T. North, a native of Leeds who had made his fortune in South American mines and then made his home in Eltham, Kent. The two men had gone to seek North's aid in providing a building for the Boys' Modern Day School. They had good reason to expect that their suit would be granted, for the man that some might have snubbed as nouveau riche – and that he undeniably was – had shown himself to be a true

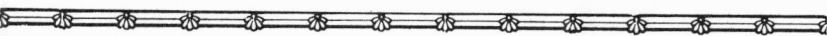

philanthropist many times in the past, financing other local ventures, such as the infirmary and the Yorkshire College. When in the course of the discussion North learned of the recent events concerning the ruins, he decided to attend to the matter himself and buy the abbey from Wilson and then present it to the people of his beloved Leeds. "There was no true Yorkshireman," he said, "who had the power, who would not have done for his native town what I have done...No doubt, I have been prosperous even beyond my expectation, but what was the use of having money if it was not spent in the way it should be spent."[61] It was, ultimately, provincial pride backed up by wealth that saved Kirkstall Abbey.

The late-Victorian fate of Kirkstall Abbey illustrates the ambiguous place of the Victorians' historic legacy in their capitalist, individualist society. What is most striking, indeed shocking, in this case is the commercialization of the medieval ruins. Lady Cardigan, her estate agents, and the speculators were all eager to profit from the high cultural status of antiquities by converting the historical associations and aesthetic worth of the abbey directly into market value. Yet the proceedings described also suggest that it is a mistake to contend that there was necessarily an adversary relationship between capitalism and historic preservation. If capitalist greed first jeopardized the integrity of Kirkstall Abbey, it was ultimately capitalist philanthropy that secured it for Leeds. Individualism also had paradoxical effects on the fate of the monastic ruins. What was at issue was who should act as the proprietors of tradition. Lady Cardigan was able to treat "the ruins of her grand old Abbey" as mere property because there were no institutional sanctions to prevent it from falling into the hands of unscrupulous speculators and no institutional channels to obviate the elaborate, chaotic private machinations of would-be preservers. The finale of the story – North's donation of the ruins to the Leeds Corporation – suggests that one answer to the problem of what was to be done with ancient buildings was collective ownership. Although laissez-faire prin-

ciples almost had disastrous results in this case, here too there is another side to the story. It is certainly an appropriate ending to this fable-like history of Victorian urban life, especially in the home town of Samuel Smiles, that it was the individual efforts of a self-made man, Colonel North, that redeemed Kirkstall Abbey, just as it was another self-made man, Colonel Akroyd, who proposed its restoration.

The case of Kirkstall Abbey is perhaps most significant in that it reveals the widespread support for historic preservation among the elites of industrial cities. The national and provincial newspapers furnish the richest documentation on this point, and they are also interesting in other respects. They reveal how the tastes and attitudes of London-based "Anti-Scrape" spread to provincial centers and show how newspapers, in turn, played their part in shaping late-Victorian attitudes toward the treatment of historic buildings. The writers who reported the remarkable story of Kirkstall Abbey venerated the ruins both as a work of art and as a cultural symbol, describing it as a "noble relic of a former age," a "revered relic of the past," and a "picturesque relic of medieval ecclesiastical architecture."[62] They agreed with "Anti-Scrape" that the threat to the medieval remains was posed on the one hand by the restorer and on the other by the speculator.[63]

The newspaper literature also illuminates the contemporary concerns the preservation of Kirkstall Abbey expressed. Of these, the most important were the needs to enhance general aesthetic appreciation and to revivify national consciousness. Both of these themes figure in a particularly suggestive article that appeared in the *Birmingham Daily Post* in August 1888, in response to the news that Kirkstall Abbey was to be disposed of on the auction block.

> A shudder must run through the mind not only of the antiquarian, but of every lover of historic art, at the announcement that Kirkstall Abbey is about to be sold by public auction. The purchaser, of course, will have the full right to do what he likes with his own, and one of the great architectural monuments

of the country will be at the mercy of any chance speculator who may think well to buy it. There ought to be some means of securing such a structure as the property of the nation, that it may be carefully preserved and left to tell its tale for future generations. We very properly purchase for our galleries and museums ancient pictures, manuscripts, and sculptures. These teach us important lessons as to the growth and development of art, and they leave in the mind permanent impressions of beauty. But there are no works which connect so immediately the life and being of old times with the evidences of its aesthetic culture, as do the great buildings which occupied the whole lives of their authors in devising and constructing. . . A national injury is committed when one of these structures is allowed to suffer from neglect, or still worse, from the hands of the ignorant restorer. The same argument applies with more force to the great monastic houses in which the religious and the social life of their communities were alike centered. The particular abbey in question is one of the oldest and most famous of such structures. Founded in the reign of STEPHEN, more than seven hundred years ago, it has stood through the most famous ages of our history, its abbots have taken their part in the national life drama that has been played; and its artistic brotherhood has embodied in enduring stone the ideas of what was to them a living art, for one of the great charms of these old buildings is that they were designed and built and modified at times when Art was really a part of the national life and an exponent of the best and deepest feelings of the people. They are, indeed, national possessions and as such ought to be preserved and protected. . .to provide for making the building accessible at all times to the people of whose history it is so picturesque an illustration.[64]

Like James Connon, this writer screened out the medieval Catholic associations of Kirkstall Abbey by emphasizing its place in English history. What is most arresting in this passage is the author's radical populist nationalism, so characteristic of late-Victorian Birmingham. For him, Kirkstall Abbey was most valuable as a grand exhibit of the quality of the old buildings "designed and built and modified at times when Art was really a part of the national life and an exponent of the best and deepest feelings of the people." He may have believed that the preservation of such remains would inspire the creation of a new art that expressed the values and aspirations of the English people.

Local newspapers also furnish invaluable evidence on the meanings, values, and functions the preservation of Kirkstall Abbey served in Leeds itself. What is most remarkable about the response of the people of this industrial city and its region to the threats to the abbey was that the major question was not *if* it should be preserved but how and by whom. There is no reason to doubt that the citizenry shared their compatriots' hope that securing the ruins would serve the twin cause of aesthetic and national education, but they also had special concerns of their own in the matter of Kirkstall Abbey. One cause its preservation served was the desire to beautify the visual environment of the industrial world. Since the early nineteenth century, the privileged residents of English cities had sought refuge from the world they had partially created by building villas in the suburbs. For those who could not afford to live in choice districts like London's Hampstead, the construction of public parks open to all was one way to satisfy the quest for *rus in urbe*, the life of the countryside within the confines of the city.[65] Hence, one citizen of Leeds, Richard Tabbern, suggested that the natural beauty of the site of Kirkstall Abbey as well as the picturesque character of the ruins might be put to very practical use. It could easily be turned into a park "which would be a constant treat to the many thousands who periodically visit the ruins from our crowded town."[66] This conception of the future of Kirkstall Abbey underlies the connection between the Victorian cults of nature and history, both of which were, on one level, quests for the picturesque.

The preservation of Kirkstall Abbey was also an expression of provincialism. Intent as Richard Tabbern was on using the grounds as a local park, he also stressed that the principal reason for saving it for Leeds was its "close identification with the history of the town."[67] It was a provincial as well as a national symbol. Councilman Alf Cooke argued that the Leeds Corporation ought to purchase it, as it was dear to all Yorkshiremen and Yorkshirewomen. Although we do not know whether he regarded it as a prospective tourist attraction that would fuel the local economy, he did say that it was so valuable that even visitors from America and the colonies traveled long distances to visit what they had always been taught to regard as one of the greatest ancient landmarks of England.[68]

The pride that inspired the campaign to save Kirkstall Abbey was closely connected to the fear of civic disgrace. "I feel sure I express the sentiments of very many, if not all," wrote one woman confidently, "when I say that the loss of so historical a building would reflect upon the taste and judgement of a town like Leeds."[69] The *Leeds Mercury* agreed: Were steps not taken to save Kirkstall Abbey, Leeds would be "justly disgraced in the estimation of the nation."[70] This view is borne out by the way several other newspapers reacted to the news that Kirkstall Abbey had been donated to Leeds by Colonel North. The *Yorkshire Evening Post* remarked that it had been "in danger of falling into speculative hands and becoming a scandal instead of an ornament to Leeds."[71] And the *Newcastle Chronicle* commented that the people of Leeds were fortunate that the abbey had not passed into "the hands of some 'nouveau riche' from the other side of the Atlantic, and become lost to the locality."[72] This is an ironic prophecy in light of the present fate of London Bridge (not the old London Bridge) adorning the deserts of Arizona. The fear of speculators is especially significant when one remembers that a "town like Leeds" and comparable northern industrial centers were severely criticized by Matthew Arnold for philistinism. Speculators, materialists devoted to doing what they like with their own property, irre-

spective of any higher values, represent a negative anima, a projection of all the characteristic flaws ascribed rightly or wrongly to the people of industrial, provincial England.

Preserving and honoring Kirkstall Abbey helped offset this inaccurate image of Leeds. What better way to publicize the town's commitment to art and history than to preserve architectural remains that had few practical uses? Certainly the appropriation of a symbol of the medieval order such as Kirkstall Abbey provided an ideal addition to the "paraphernalia of gentility." If the story of Kirkstall Abbey reveals how the cult of the past was commercialized in Victorian England, it also shows how the diffusion of the values described in this chapter furnished a way to transform, or at least polish, commercial and industrial life. Perhaps the writer in the *Metropolitan* who called Kirkstall that "useful ruin" was more correct than he had reason to know.[73] The acquisitions of the remains of the past contributed to the transformation of the image of the present.

In the summer of 1895, the grounds of Kirkstall Abbey were finally reopened to the public. All had not gone smoothly in the days that followed Colonel North's presentation of the ruins to the Leeds Corporation, but unfortunately there is limited documentary evidence on the actual work done.[74] Yet we know that its basic aim was to preserve Kirkstall Abbey's character as a ruin rather than to restore it to its "original design" or make it into a usable church, as George Gilbert Scott had planned. Not everyone was satisfied with the results of the work undertaken by the architect, J. T. Mickelthwaite. Some objected to the fact that in stripping ivy from the abbey walls to prevent further corrosion, he robbed it of much of its picturesque quality.[75] And there were complaints of a more general nature: An architect designated by the SPAB noted that although some of the work was necessary, some was unnecessary and some very objectionable. The abbey, apparently, had to be protected even from its admirers.[76]

On the day of the opening ceremonies, however, dissension was forgotten. Although the townspeople had come to pay

Kirkstall Abbey.

The Bishop of Ripon delivering the Address

The reopening of Kirkstall Abbey, 1895. (By permission of The Illustrated London News *Picture Library.)*

tribute to the remnants of the past, they also emphasized its functions in the present. The mayor of Leeds remarked that the purchase and repair of Kirkstall Abbey proved that "Leeds was not without men who entertained strong regard for the landmarks of the historic past...which were as beacons set upon a hill to guide the present and the future." The "venerable relic" that had cost Colonel North at least ten thousand pounds to buy and the Leeds Corporation between five and six thousand pounds to refurbish was now regarded as a treasure by the townspeople and would be guarded as such for posterity. At least one writer who covered the ceremonies for a local newspaper was impressed by the unprecedented and unique character of the enterprise: Leeds was the first municipal corporation to care for a monastic ruin. Even in their encounter with history, the citizens of Leeds were innovators. Fascinating as was the story of the donation of Kirkstall Abbey by the powerful Norman baron Henry de Lacy, it was not "nearly so fascinating as the latter-day romance of this poor son of Leeds, going forth in quest of fortune, and coming back with riches and generous impulse enough to work out so noble a benefaction."[77] Here, as elsewhere, Victorians drew modern morals from medieval mysteries.

The city churches, York

The train that took the enthusiastic sightseers of the Yorkshire Archaeological and Topographical Society from Leeds to York on 19 July 1874 was, on one level, a time machine that transported them from the heart of the modern industrial world to the most medieval of English cities. Despite the geographical proximity of the two places, they presented an almost perfect contrast in economy and social structure, in townscape and life-style. It would have been unthinkable for Edward Freeman and William Hunt to omit York from their series on *Historic Towns*.[78] Its heyday had been in the Middle Ages, when it was a center of the wool trade in addition to being the major northern seat of ecclesiastical and secular administration. This golden age, however, proved relatively ephemeral, for Leeds's status and wealth declined as that of York grew. By the first decades of the nineteenth century this inequality was particularly striking: Whereas Leeds and the other towns of the West Riding expanded enormously during this period, York's growth, although respectable, was disconcertingly meager when seen against the foil of its newly affluent neighbors. Like many other historic towns, York never industrialized. Its economy rested – all too much – on handicraft and retailing operations throughout the nineteenth century. Although the advent of the railway helped reestablish York as a market center, this only partially mitigated the sense of social stagnation.[79]

There were other reasons why York deserved the name of historic town. It was an immovable feast for the lover of art and history, because it was as rich in ancient survivals as it was poor in industrial technology. Its aesthetic virtues and its social deficiencies were closely related: Precisely because York was, so to speak, off the map of modernization, it retained the visual splendor that delighted the starving eyes of Victorian city dwellers. Industrialization made the townscape of York seem all the more distinctive because it was dominated by the spires of churches, whereas the chimneys of factories ruled in Leeds. As such, it attracted the attention and admiration of Victorian tourists like the Yorkshire Archaeological and Topographical Society. The people of York, like those of other historic towns, compensated for their minor role in the march of improvement by stressing the glories of their past. Its architectural remains and their historical associations were celebrated by historians and guidebook writers and excavated by antiquarians and archeologists.[80] Alderman Sir James Meek, for instance, reminded the Yorkshire archeologists that "deep in the twilight of far antiquity . . . York was a seat of empire" and that "almost every foot of ground here was hallowed with historic interest."[81]

The historic interest of York also provided the theme of another speech delivered to the Yorkshire archeologists during their 1874 excursion. The speaker was William Thomson,

The historic riches of York. Engraving from The Graphic, *1881. (By permission of* The Illustrated London News *Picture Library.)*

the archbishop of York and honorary president of the society's East Riding branch. He emphasized the obligations of the people of York to their historic city.

> To take the study of monuments...it would be a shameful thing if they in the city of York – standing upon ground every inch of which was, as it were, consecrated by memories of the past – should know nothing of the soil on which they trod. People might have a vague, general idea that the Romans were once in York, and that there were abbeys until they were destroyed; but they owed to the soil much more respectful attention than that. They ought not to possess so vast a treasure-house without doing something to make themselves much better acquainted with it, and without tracing what those fragments – upon which time had laid so heavy a hand – meant in the past, what they taught now, and what was their lesson for the future. This was a positive duty. They were almost like the custodians of a great museum – custodians of a singularly valuable collection of antiquities. If any one of them had come into possession, by bequest or otherwise, of such a collection, he would be ashamed not to be able to give some account to his friends and neighbours of the rare things he possessed. In that point of view the people of Yorkshire, and of York in particular, were bound to devote some attention to this study, because their soil was covered with most interesting relics – on the ground, under the ground, and all about them, belonging to every age of England's past, throwing light upon both its civil and its ecclesiastical history.[82]

The archbishop's remarks are supremely ironic in light of an action he engineered some years later. In February 1885, he released the report of a committee he chaired, supposedly composed of persons representing a wide range of viewpoints. Charged with the task of evaluating the state of the church in York

and, in particular, with considering the rearrangement of parish boundaries, they investigated how to make the church a more effective institution. The report – which, incidentally, did not enjoy the unanimous approval of the committee's members – noted that the parish structure of York was substantially the same as it had been since the Reformation, when existing arrangements were last dramatically altered. But massive shifts in population, such as the growth of suburbs and especially the split between Anglicans and Dissenters, made these boundaries obsolete and counterproductive. The difficulty was that in a parish of four thousand, for example, perhaps two thousand or more attended chapel, leaving the pews of Anglican congregations half empty. Although a small parish was in and of itself an evil to the mind of His Grace, this evil was aggravated by the fact that certain parishes' endowments were so small as to render the churches insupportably uneconomical. The report recommended combining certain congregations, because reducing the number of benefices from twenty-six to twenty would enable the church to improve the livings of the incumbents as well as to provide for the construction of new churches in the suburbs. The churches involved included St. Crux; St. John, Ousebridge; St. Martin-cum-Gregory; St. Mary's Bishophill Junior; and Holy Trinity, Goodramgate. The report was extremely vague on what was to be done with these churches. But it did note that they were to be "disused, prior to subsequent removal" – a colorless bureaucratic phrase that veiled the intention of destroying some of the churches, transporting others to new sites, and using still others for school or parish purposes.[83]

To understand the plan and the controversy it caused, it is useful to consider its author. Born in 1819 and educated at Shrewsbury and Queen's College, Oxford, William Thomson was as untouched by the Oxford movement in young adulthood as by ritualism in middle age. He adhered to his early formed opinions as rigidly as they adhered to him, retaining his predominantly Low Church evangelical bent throughout his life. Logical, pragmatic, individualistic, he was an exceptionally able administrator. These characteristics manifested

St. Mary's Bishophill Junior, 1966. (By permission of the National Monuments Record.)

Holy Trinity, Good-ramgate. (By permission of the National Monuments Record.)

themselves in his decision to restructure the parish arrangements of York. When the report was released, he stressed that having served as the archbishop of York for twenty years, he was no revolutionary. But insisting that he hoped to keep "ancient arrangements" as much as possible could not mitigate the radicalism of his scheme. It was nothing if not ironic in view of his professed veneration of antiquities and dedication to archeology. And it was all the more ironic because if many archbishops were eager to restore medieval churches, few were willing to dispose of them. That he held to his plan as long as he did despite growing public criticism was symptomatic of his general truculence. Never fully accepted either

118

by the clergy or the laity of York despite his long service there, he compensated by being unduly assertive and overly defensive.[84] These qualities almost resulted in the destruction of some of the town's loveliest old churches.

The medieval churches in question were valuable both for their historical associations and their aesthetic qualities. They were, for the most part, built in the Perpendicular style. St. Michael's, Spurriergate, had been donated by William the Conqueror to St. Mary's Abbey and was frequently referred to in the old records that Victorians so relished publishing. St. Mary's Bishophill Junior, a graceful union of Saxon and Norman work, was thought to contain the oldest extant architecture in York.

Another church that dated back to the conquest, St. Cuthbert's, had recently attracted attention because archeologists had discovered Roman antiquities on its site. The Church of St. Helen, according to tradition, stood on the foundation of a temple once dedicated to the pagan goddess Diana and was also associated with the Emperor Constantine. Vandalizing this particular church seems to have been something of a local tradition: First defaced in 1547 by citizens who found its location inconvenient, as it prevented easy access through York's winding streets, it bore the cross of restoration throughout the nineteenth century. Of all the churches, St. Crux was the most notable, because of its beauty and its memorials.[85]

The dilemmas of the York city churches and Kirkstall Abbey present marked contrasts. Whereas Kirkstall Abbey was in ruins and was, therefore, useless in practical terms long before the campaign to save it began, the York city churches were still in use but were quickly becoming obstacles to progress. Whereas Kirkstall Abbey was privately owned, the York city churches were, of course, ecclesiastical possessions. Whereas the problem with Kirkstall Abbey was who should purchase the ruins and how it should be cared for, the question with York city churches was how to save the redundant edifices from demolition. And whereas the danger to Kirkstall Abbey came from greedy speculators, the threat to the York city churches stemmed from an enlightened archbishop and his supporters.

The late-Victorian history of the York city churches exemplifies how social forces endangered the safety of historic survivals. It was demographic shifts and inadequate funds that first rendered the churches redundant. Although there is little evidence to suggest that the archbishop and his allies cherished them for either their historic or aesthetic value, or even for their religious associations, there is likewise little reason to believe that their decision was anything but a pragmatic, utilitarian one. The efficacy of the church seemed more pressing than the integrity of its houses of worship. Apart from changing patterns of population, the churches' fates were uncertain because, unlike Kirkstall Abbey, which was located on

the outskirts of Leeds, they were situated variously throughout the city center. It was, therefore, especially difficult for York to live comfortably with these survivals, because of the lack of space. As Canon James Raine put it: "Every day the present is swallowing up the past . . . we advance, so rapidly, we make so many changes, that there seems to be no room for the present and past together."[86]

Protests against the plan's flagrant disregard for the value of the medieval churches began soon after the report was publicized. The Reverend Newton Mant, vicar of a church in Sledmere, a neighboring village of York, who was also a corresponding member of the SPAB in the North Riding, quickly informed the organization's secretary, Thackeray Turner, of the imminent danger to the churches. What is most striking is that although Mant was an Anglican minister, his interest in the fate of the city churches was in no sense religious. "I care little," he insisted, "for the ecclesiastical aspect of the question. I should not much object to the use of the churches as schools if desirable, but we must all object to their destruction."[87] Although he valued the historical associations of the churches, his concern with their preservation was essentially aesthetic. In his letter to Turner, for instance, he commented in passing about the beauty of the churches, referring in particular to the "picturesque church of St. John on the Ouse," the "graceful front and belfry of St. Helen's," and the "interesting early tower" of St. Mary's Bishophill.

Mant, who proved himself to be an acute observer and a canny politician in the controversy that followed, correctly identified the two major obstacles that faced the preservers in this case. "The whole question in York is entangled (as usual)," he asserted, "in a web of personal, local and financial interests."[88] What is more, Mant had no doubt that it was the archbishop himself who had spun the web and ensured its tightness. Mant disliked the prelate, but if he was neither temperate nor tolerant in his accusations of insincerity and hypocrisy, he respected Thomson's shrewdness and his posi-

tion.[89] He was well aware that the archbishop's sponsorship of the plan made all the difference in its reception, effectively inhibiting opposition from many clergymen, some of whom stood to benefit from it financially. The second difficulty was not malice but ignorance. Mant thought the people of York distressingly philistine in their blindness to the artistic and historic worth of the churches in their midst. He concluded that the only way to save the churches would be to create a "great stir," for only this would force the archbishop, who was afraid of public opinion, to reconsider his scheme.[90]

The first efforts of the SPAB, directed by Mant, went into recruiting the support of local clergymen for their protest campaign. Nowhere was the web of local influence more obvious than among the clergy of York, who, quite naturally, feared offending an archbishop known neither for the quantity nor the quality of his mercy. Yet this is not to say that all those who supported the plan did so only for fear of earthly retribution. The Reverend George Trundle, for instance, would surely have never been tried for sentimental or intellectual attachment to art and history. When asked by the society for his assistance, he replied by reaffirming his loyalty to His Grace and his plan, stressing that he particularly liked the idea of using the old churches for building material. Quite literally, he believed that the old should serve as the foundation for the new. Although he had no objection to the disuse or destruction of the churches, he wanted to ensure that their sacred sites be kept untouched and uncorrupted by secular or commercial ventures.[91]

Other clerics were silent purely because they had no desire to oppose the archbishop. Of these, the most remarkable example is Canon James Raine, a local archeologist and historian of some repute and standing in York, whose assistance would have been valuable indeed to the preservers' cause. He had been a member of the archbishop's committee and there had opposed the plan, but after the decision was made he was reticent to take any further action. His passivity was particularly ironic because it was Raine who later wrote the volume on *York* for the *Historic Towns* series. In an effort to rouse the

"supine archeologist" from his convenient, if understandable, slumber, the SPAB printed a circular with excerpts of his previous condemnations of the destruction of ancient buildings in York. Whether Raine was indeed "touched to the quick" by this move is difficult to say, but at any rate it seems he was not sufficiently touched to take an active part in the campaign.[92] Among the clergymen who did were the Reverend T.W. Norwood, a corresponding member of the SPAB; the Reverend S. H. Bennett, vicar of St. Mary's Bishophill Junior, which was threatened by the archbishop's scheme; and the Reverend Arthur J. Munby, the retired vicar of Hovingham, who proved to be an especially valuable ally.[93] These men, and Newton Mant above all, were instrumental in shaping public opinion in York, especially among their parishioners. There is little evidence to suggest that the position York clergymen took on the fate of the city churches reflected theological differences, though local ecclesiastical conflicts almost inevitably manifested themselves in the controversy.

The early months of the campaign to save the city churches are of special interest in two respects. In the first place, the SPAB offered its usual arguments in defense of historic preservation. The prospect of destroying a group of medieval churches that reflected the changing styles of English life and art enraged Thackeray Turner and his fellows. He summed up the organization's viewpoint in a letter to the *Yorkshire Post*: "It simply wishes to state, that the proposal is, in its opinion, disgraceful. The scheme treats these medieval buildings as if they were so much old building material instead of as valuable works of art." No doubt, the plan would incur the disapproval of the nation, "for no matter whether a man values them as works of art, as works of antiquity, or as religious monuments, he will be equally offended by their demolition."[94] He proceeded to argue his case by commenting on the historical associations and aesthetic character of the churches.

Second, as the preservers tried to convince the townspeople of the importance of protecting the city churches, they received renewed proof that the treatment of ancient buildings was closely tied to existing power structures, the "web of

influence" that Mant decried. Much of this complicated, confused controversy revolved around determining precisely what the archbishop and his allies intended to do with the churches. At the beginning of their campaign, the SPAB tried to convince W. W. Hargrove, the editor of the *York Herald*, who had been a member of the archbishop's committee, to use his influence to help save the churches, or at least to allow the society to use his newspaper to publicize their viewpoint. In response, he stressed that like his father before him – who, incidentally, had published York guidebooks that described the historical riches of the town in detail – he took the greatest interest in the historical antiquity of York, always condemning unnecessary destruction of its architectural survivals. But in this instance there was no need to worry, for the SPAB had misconstrued the situation. There was, he maintained, no intention of destroying the churches. The only reason that the report mentioned "disuse, prior to subsequent removal" was that it was to serve as the foundation for a bill that the archbishop intended to introduce into Parliament – a bill that was to give him adequate latitude to deal with the churches as he thought appropriate. In any case, the fate of each church would be considered individually, and wherever feasible the buildings would be preserved for school or parish purposes.[95] Not only Hargrove but Archbishop Thomson himself summarily denied any allegation of the impending demolition of the city churches. Responding to the inquiries of such notables as Lord Herries and Lord Percy, both of whom were deeply dismayed by news of the scheme, he told them to put their minds at rest.[96]

Was the threat to the York city churches, then, a mere bogey? There is, of course, no foolproof way to probe the archbishop's intentions, especially because his private secretary saw fit to destroy the greater part of Thomson's correspondence – an act that hardly inspires confidence. Yet there is little reason to believe – and as the controversy went on it seems that few did believe – that the committee's plan was as innocent as they maintained. When protests began, Hargrove, for example, speedily backtracked, first contending that the

churches were not to be harmed, then saying that the affair was not the concern of the SPAB, and finally complaining that the cost of caring for every scrap of antiquity in York would be prohibitive.[97] The contradiction between the report and the version of it later propagated is particularly glaring because it was Hargrove's newspaper, the *York Herald*, that served as one of the preservers' major sources of information. The controversy soon became an increasingly acrimonious fight in which each side accused the other of dishonesty and hypocrisy. Thackeray Turner, for example, whose wit apparently sometimes vanquished his sense of tact, wrote a letter to local newspapers in which he highlighted the ironic spectacle of an iconoclastic archbishop, a churchman who was a wanton destroyer of the memorials of art and history.[98]

To dramatize their cause, the SPAB decided to hold a public meeting in York at the end of May 1885. The elaborate forethought that went into planning even the smallest details of the meeting is typical of the politics of preservation. Newton Mant hoped that the gathering, which was to be held at the Corn Exchange, would attract professionals and tradespeople, clergymen and churchwardens.[99] To counteract the mistaken impression – which had been deliberately created by the archbishop's forces – that the preservers' campaign was a thinly disguised High Church plot by a High Church society to discredit His Grace – they decided to have both a High Church and a Low Church speaker attend. Also in full view was to be a native son of Yorkshire, who was to act as living proof that the preservers were not, as their enemies contended, Londoners intent on belittling and disgracing the people of York. Even the presence of William Morris was carefully considered. At first, Mant feared that his radical politics might antagonize the audience, but soon he found himself faced with a rather different dilemma: publicizing Morris's identity, as few had heard of him. Finally, he reckoned that Morris would be a "good draw."[100] Mant was careful to warn his compatriots that on this occasion they must get their facts exactly right, for any inaccuracy would be seized upon by their opponents as proof that they misunderstood the situation. Above all, they

had to avoid giving the impression of any personal animosity toward the archbishop. "All opposition," the vicar insisted, "must be made on historical, artistic and antiquarian grounds."

The York meeting is most significant because it illuminates the contemporary concerns that the preservation of the city churches expressed. The various spokesmen for the SPAB stressed different aspects of their aesthetic and historic worth. Opening the proceedings, Richard C. Grosvenor, a Grosvenor of Mayfair, forcefully struck the keynote. Although he was neither an archeologist nor an architect, he felt great veneration for works of ancient art of every kind. Their preservation was of far more importance than all the gold, silver, and dross of modern life. Popplewell Pullan, the representative of the Royal Archaeological Institute, pointed out that he could find no parallel in all history to this horrendous scheme. The churches were particularly valuable because their Perpendicular style was preeminently English. Saving them, therefore, was an expression of national pride. Tempest Anderson, who was obviously influenced by William Morris, contended that the churches should be cherished as symbols of preindustrial art. They were "remnants of a period before competition, piecework and contracts brought everything down to the level of machinery." And Morris himself added that their small size was no true index of the value of churches like St. Crux, which contained some of the most exquisite stained glass he had ever seen. Its antiquities alone had made York a pilgrimage place for the entire world. Without them York would be a very commonplace city indeed.[101]

What Morris recognized was that the destruction of the city churches would disrupt the visual identity of York. To underline the importance of this point he and his colleagues appealed to the townspeople's civic pride and to their fear of disgrace – themes that had proved so important in the campaign to save Kirkstall Abbey. Richard Grosvenor warned that the destruction of the city churches would inflict a blow upon education, history, and culture that would discredit York, and with good reason, in the eye of a watchful nation. C. L. Wood put it well when he said that "without them York would not

be York." A similar point had been made some months earlier in an interesting letter to the local press. Responding to the proposal of removing several of the churches from their present sites to other parts of York, "Rusticus," as he called himself, argued:

> The idea of removing old churches without doing them damage is absurd. They were built for different sites, and for their own surroundings they are especially suited... You could no more reproduce Holy Trinity in another spot than you could set up Humpty Dumpty on his wall after his fateful tumble. You might build up a 19th century forgery, and with enough money make it as big and ghastly as the new church for which Holy Trinity has been forsaken, but the reinsertion of a window here and a table there, would be no true preservation of art and history... York is the most picturesque city in the three kingdoms, but man, not nature, has made York what she is. If her citizens value cheaply or destroy the art of the past, let them clearly remember that, as yet, they have nothing as good to put in its place.[102]

Because the city churches were fundamental to the sense of place, their preservation was imperative.

The York meeting is also noteworthy in other respects. First, the counterarguments put forth by the archbishop's supporters reveal that sometimes even those who advocated the disuse or destruction of historic buildings took care to express their veneration of the past. S. W. North, for instance, was not to be surpassed in his devotion to history. He told the audience that he revered every stone of the ancient city that has been consecrated by the use of ages and the kinship of generations. That he used the purplish, quasireligious language of the cult of the past underlines the prestige historic survivals had in Victorian culture. It also shows how deceptive such rhetoric could be. Second, the debate between the proponents and opponents of the plan underlines the fact that if historic preservation served certain contemporary needs, at the same time it impeded oth-

ers. S. W. North argued that the ecclesiastical authorities had the right to treat the city churches as they saw fit, because the necessities of the living were more important than the honor paid to the dead. Cobden-Sanderson responded that he too believed that the living must have priority, and that was precisely why he hoped to save the places where they experienced the highest sentiments. The local audience, evidently, agreed. At the end of the meeting they endorsed overwhelmingly the motion protesting the proposed demolition of the churches.[103]

Although the finale of the meeting demonstrates the triumph of the SPAB's ideals, their victory did not empower them to decree how the churches were to be treated. The following week proved particularly eventful. The churchwardens of St. Mary's Bishophill Junior decided that it was to be kept in use after all. But this victory was offset by the news that the fund for restoring St. Crux, then a virtual ruin, was to be returned to the donors and that the plan for rebuilding the church was to be dispensed with. Hearing the news, Richard Grosvenor complained to Thackeray Turner that despite their efforts, "nothing short of hanging the Archbishop and his allies would be of any public utility now as far as the York City Churches are concerned."[104]

There was less reason for despair than Grosvenor knew. The archbishop was being hung, albeit metaphorically, in the press. Not that all opinion condemned him. "The issue," it was argued in *Truth*, for instance, was not so "much of sentiment as of pounds, shillings and pence."[105] But in general the nation proved, at least in rhetoric, that sometimes cultural ideals could triumph over material considerations. Here again, the press campaign was a powerful way to spread the gospel of preservationism as well as to pressure those in power. The archbishop was indicted, and his scheme criticized, by both the secular and the ecclesiastical press.[106] Of all the exchanges, the most telling, as well as the most bitter, took place between Archbishop Thomson and Lord Percy. Percy, the president of the Royal Archaeological Institute, made repeated protests to, and then about, the archbishop, who in turn became in-

creasingly angered by these "assaults on his character." Their correspondence, which was eventually published in the *Times* and other newspapers, marked the public culmination of the controversy.[107] Finally, in September, the archbishop bowed to public pressure and assured Percy that no harm would come to the buildings.

And thus the York city churches were saved.

The studies in this chapter reveal how difficult it was for Victorians to reconcile the sword with which they protected the survivals of their ancestors and the trowel with which they built a new world. Given the intense social pressures they faced, it is not surprising that they were often ambivalent about the treatment of historic buildings despite their veneration of the past. The compromise they developed was to preserve a limited number of highly symbolic ancient buildings. This strategy was not without its contradictions. Although the SPAB wanted to preserve the additions and revisions that Tudor architects, for instance, made to medieval buildings, they would not extend the same right to Victorian architects. Anyone who examines the barbaric restorations of Westminster Abbey or St. Albans' Cathedral can appreciate their decision. But by granting ancient buildings the quasireligious status of virtually untouchable places, they deprived them of their mundane functions. Although neither William Morris nor Frederic Harrison wanted to turn them into "in situ" museums, all too often this is what happened. Since the 1960s, many architects and planners have tried to approach the problem of what to do with historic buildings by finding new uses for their old fabrics.[108]

Whatever its shortcomings, historic preservation helped to satisfy Victorians' search for aesthetic, provincial, and national symbols. It seems likely that Victorians who rarely reflected on the historic or aesthetic value of ancient buildings protested when they were threatened because destroying them would disrupt the sense of place. Without Kirkstall Abbey, Leeds would not have been Leeds any more than York would

have been York without its city churches. In an age of radical social and environmental disruptions, the preservation of familiar landmarks helped satisfy deep-seated needs for stability and orientation. The paradox is that in a world of change, even ruins could serve as symbols of continuity as well as evanescence.

Not content merely with exploring, collecting, and preserving medieval remains, Victorians delighted in rehabilitating historic forms to suit their own purposes. The preservation of ancient buildings was no substitute for creating a functional, beautiful architecture that expressed contemporary values and aspirations. To study this quest for a civic and aesthetic style we must move from Yorkshire to Lancashire.

4

The architecture
of the industrial city

Trade has now a chivalry of its own; a chivalry whose
stars are radiant with the more benignant lustre of
justice, happiness and religion, and whose titles will
outlive the barbarous nomenclature of Charlemagne.
– Henry Dunckley, *The Charter of the Nations* (1854)

Architecture has a noble and lofty office to perform
...Besides ministering to our comforts and satisfying
our material wants – besides pleasing the eye and
embellishing our cities – architecture has to raise up
monuments which may tell to future ages of our
habits of thought, of our governing or prompting ideas,
and of our state of civilization...It is the duty of our
architecture to translate our character into stone.
– *Building News* (1858)

Medievalism in Manchester

In the 1840s, Manchester was swamped with slums, smoke,
and factories as well as by distinguished visitors anxious to
inspect the "shock city of the industrial revolution"; yet by
the 1890s the face of the Lancashire capital was perhaps most
remarkable for its neomedieval features. If, for instance, a
fashionable young architect from Hampstead, a partisan of the
Queen Anne style, visited Manchester in 1900 to meet a prospective client, he would have been impressed – and as a
self-styled anti-Victorian rebel, depressed – by the bevy of
high-Victorian Gothic buildings that pervaded the city.

Spiraling towers and pointed arches became fundamental
aspects of the visual identity of Manchester. As the architect
walked around the city center, among the major Victorian
Gothic buildings he would have seen were Thomas Worthington's
Police Courts, Minshull Street (1868), and Alfred Waterhouse's
Prudential Assurance Company (1881) as well as Edward
Salomons's Reform Club (1870), both of which were located

on King Street. From there it was only a short walk to one of the most impressive buildings in Manchester, the John Rylands Library, Deansgate (1890–9), which was the last major work of the secular Gothic Revival in England, and undoubtedly one of the finest. Sponsored by the wife of the textile manufacturer whose name it bore, it was, as its iconography announced, a "cathedral of learning" that soon built up a great collection of medieval manuscripts. There was no better place for our architect to observe the passion for neomedieval forms than the Albert Square. There three works of Thomas Worthington – the Albert Memorial (1862), the Memorial Hall (1865), and the Bridgewater Buildings (1864) – provided an ideal setting for Alfred Waterhouse's Manchester Town Hall (1868–77). If the triumph of the Gothic Revival was most striking in the city center, it was not confined to it. To the north, on Great Ducie Street, was Waterhouse's Venetian Gothic Assize Courts (1859), the first major work of the secular Gothic Revival in Manchester. To the south was yet another of Waterhouse's works, Owens College, Oxford Road (1870). To the west were George Edmund Street's St. Peter, Swinton (1868), and George Frederick Bodley's St. Augustine, Pendlebury (1870). And to the east were still more Neo-Gothic churches: William Butterfield's St. Cross, Ashton Road (1863), Edward Pugin's St. Francis, Gorton (1863), and George Gilbert Scott's Christ Church, Denton (1853).[1] All these buildings created a sense of the past in one of the major citadels of modernity.

Medievalism in Manchester! The combination is particularly suggestive because in the 1840s Manchester was seen as the representative city of the new industrial age. For its celebrants, the phenomenal wealth and growth of Manchester proved that laissez-faire individualism, technological ingenuity, and industrial capitalism led to freedom, progress, and affluence. But its critics contended that in Manchester industrialization had led to the degradation of the working class, the construction of a formless, ugly town, and the glorification of a materialistic attitude so enamored of fact that it had no appreciation of fancy.[2] That the Gothic Revival flourished in Manchester, whose early nineteenth-century leaders directed much of their

awesome energy toward obliterating the anachronistic survivals of the "feudal" social order, underscores the paradoxical presence of medievalism in modernity. The visual transformation of Manchester through the adaptation of Gothic forms demonstrates dramatically that medievalism was part and parcel of the improving, industrializing society of Victorian England.

Although it would be difficult to overestimate the significance of medievalism in Manchester, at the same time it is necessary to interpret it cautiously. It is important to remember that when Manchester went medieval, as it were, it was neither a "shock city" nor the most advanced city in England. Manchester was, however, still one of the major cities that epitomized the values and structures of liberal industrial England. And it must also be kept in mind that there was no carefully conceived master plan behind the triumph of Gothic in Manchester. Fashionable as Gothic certainly was, decisions on the style of particular buildings were made on pragmatic as well as aesthetic and symbolic grounds. Yet if the pervasive taste for Gothic was no more planned than the spatial segregation that concealed the squalors of the slums from the sensitive eyes of the middle classes, here too, as we will see, there are significant patterns.

The Town Hall is the best place to study the meanings and functions of medievalism in Manchester, because it was the "architectural and municipal center" of the town. This civic symbol was "fashioned like a cathedral" and was seen as an "expression of the spirit of the town."[3] It is located in the Albert Square and is oriented sideways in relation to the surrounding streets of the main district of Manchester. By the time the construction of the building began in 1868, the Albert Square already boasted several examples of neomedieval design: notably, Worthington's shrinelike memorial to the Prince Consort and his Memorial Hall and Bridgewater Buildings, both of which were Venetian Gothic. The Early English Gothic forms and immense scale of Waterhouse's Town Hall tend to dwarf the surrounding buildings, thus emphasizing the monumental character of the edifice that John Bright called a "municipal palace."

The Manchester New Town Hall, circa late nineteenth century. (By permission of the Manchester Public Library.)

The Town Hall was built with brick encased in Spinkwell stone, because this light-brown material, which came from quarries near Bradford, seemed most likely to resist discoloration from the foul fumes of industry. The shape of the building is a triangle that initially appears irregular but is actually symmetrical. It is between three and four hundred feet long on each side and nearly comes to a point at its southern extremity on Cooper Street. All in all, it covers 8,648 square yards. The principal facade, the Albert Square front, is entirely symmetrical except for slight differences in the arrangement

The Manchester New Town Hall. Engraving from The Graphic, *14 October 1876.
(By permission of* The Illustrated London News *Picture Library.)*

of the windows. Immediately behind the projecting gable of this facade rises the building's most striking feature, a clock tower, which symbolized civic pride to Victorians as well as to the burghers of the Middle Ages and the Renaissance. What is most striking about the Princess Street and Lloyd Street fronts is that Waterhouse broke up their wall planes and skylines to such an extent that the *Builder* remarked that they were more like "a collection of buildings on one block" than a continuous, unified design. This treatment was justified because there was "little more than a street's breadth to afford a view of the building."[4] More important, it points to the picturesque aesthetic that informed the Town Hall. Alfred Waterhouse advised young architects "to take care lest a design prove to be anything but a pleasure to the eye" and to attend to "the outline seen against the sky."[5] The beautiful silhouette of the Town Hall, especially attractive at night, reveals that he followed his own counsel. The architectural richness of the building served social as well as aesthetic functions: It proclaimed unabashedly the wealth of the city. Its floors were graced by marble mosaics in a variety of colors, every swirl of which attested to the prosperity of Manchester. Certainly the building was visibly and aggressively the best that money could buy – approximately one million pounds worth.[6]

The Town Hall, although based on medieval forms, was essentially a modern building. In 1877, precisely nine years after he had been declared the winner of the Town Hall competition, Alfred Waterhouse described his work in a paper delivered to the Royal Institute of British Architects. Professor T. L. Donaldson, a past president of the organization, who had been one of the contest's assessors, congratulated Waterhouse on the final result. He declared that it was an excellent example of "medieval gothic architecture." Although Waterhouse graciously accepted his praise, he also asserted that the building was "essentially adapted to the wants of the present day."[7] He was not alone in his estimation. William Axon, a Manchester Liberal, who compiled an introductory architectural and historical sketch of the building for the opening ceremonies argued that "the style of the New Town Hall may

136

*Interior view of the
Manchester New Town
Hall. (By permission of
the Manchester Public
Library.)*

The surroundings of the Manchester New Town Hall. Engraving from The Graphic, 14 October 1876. (By permission of The Illustrated London News Picture Library.)

best be described as thirteenth century Gothic suffused with the feeling and spirit of the present age. It is a successful vindication of the claim of Gothic to be capable of serving all the purposes of the practical life of the nineteenth century."[8] The *Builder* praised "the style of modernised and municipalised Gothic which Mr. Waterhouse to a great extent invented or developed for himself."[9]

The Town Hall was a high-Victorian Gothic building in more than name. First, Alfred Waterhouse was typical of high-Victorian Goths in that he abandoned the religiously inspired, religiously pure imitation of medieval architectural forms characteristic of early Victorian architects, especially those build-

138

ing under Anglican or Catholic banners. Although medieval architecture provided his models, he did not try to imitate it precisely. What Waterhouse said of his Assize Courts holds true for his Town Hall: "Whenever I thought that the particular object in view could not be best obtained by a strict obedience to precedent, I took the liberty of departing from it."[10] He attended to the functional aspects of the building no less than to the "outline seen against the sky." Throughout the Town Hall he employed the most sophisticated technology available. There was nothing at all medieval, for instance, in the heating system of the building.[11] Known as a superb planner, he carefully designed the building to serve the needs of that preeminently modern entity, a burgeoning bureaucracy, whose purview and divisions mirrored growing social and administrative specialization and control. Within the Neo-Gothic facade, the town council and a wide range of municipal departments, including Gas, Health, Water, Housing, Paving and Highways, Markets, Scavenging, and Hackney Coaches, attempted to manage the practical affairs of Manchester. The architect placed the offices along continuous corridors to permit maximum redistribution of space among the various departments with a minimum of structural change. The Town Hall was a civic symbol, but it was a symbol to work in. If its historicist form and its pragmatic functions were, in a sense, opposites, at the same time these extremes met and married in this, as in countless other examples of Victorian architecture.

The Town Hall must be understood in its aesthetic context. The late date of the building – its cornerstone was laid in 1868 and it was finally opened to an admiring public in 1877 – is itself suggestive. It reminds us that the building belongs to the final act of the Gothic Revival and not to its early phases. Along with Street's Law Courts (1874–82), Waterhouse's Town Hall represented the culmination of secular Neo-Gothic architecture. The irony is that although both works demonstrated that medieval forms were adaptable to modern functional requirements, by the time they were completed the Gothic Revival had largely run its course. The Queen Anne style dominated the English imagination in the last decades of the nineteenth century.

The Manchester Town Hall was one of a cluster of Neo-Gothic municipal buildings erected in English cities in the Victorian age. If the Gothic Revival was, in its early phases, largely the cultural preserve of upper-class Anglican England, in its last phases it assumed a distinctly, if not exclusively, northern accent. Among the Neo-Gothic public buildings constructed in industrial Lancashire and Yorkshire from approximately 1860 to 1890 were the Bradford Wool Exchange (1864–7), the Bradford Town Hall (1873), the Barrow-in-Furness Town Hall (1882–7), and the Middlesbrough Town Hall (1883–9). Another impressive index of the victory of Gothic is the fact that the majority of buildings built during Joseph Chamberlain's mayoralty in Birmingham were Gothic.[12]

The vogue of Gothic in secular architecture represented a major shift in Victorian taste. Although early Victorians turned to Gothic for their national symbol, the Houses of Parliament, in general they preferred to use the classical style for their public buildings, for it evoked thoughts of representative government and antique grandeur; Gothic, which summoned forth thoughts of ecclesiastical piety and tradition, was reserved for their churches. But by the 1850s this aesthetic etiquette had broken down. Gothic architecture became fashionable because, as the completed Houses of Parliament demonstrated, it was adaptable to contemporary functional requirements, it satisfied the desire for picturesque facades and silhouettes, and it was historically associated with the development of national, religious, and commercial life.[13]

The story of the making of the Manchester Town Hall provides an excellent case study of the place of medievalism in the industrial world. It illuminates how Victorians appropriated medieval aesthetic models to create a distinctive architectural style and how they preempted historic figures, forms, and symbols to define, celebrate, and defend their traditions.

The search for a style

In its origins as well as in its scale, the Town Hall reflected the phenomenal development of Victorian Manchester. Not

the least impressive sign of the growth of the city as well as its bureaucracy was that Waterhouse's Town Hall was the second municipal edifice that Manchester built in the course of the nineteenth century. That it succeeded a classical building on King Street designed by the local architect Francis Goodwin (1825) reflects a fundamental change in taste. The New Town Hall was, indirectly, the child of the cotton famine. As the Manchester Corporation expanded its scope to cope with the enormous social problems the famine caused, it proved necessary to rent additional office space in buildings adjacent to the old town hall. Manchester had outgrown itself. Although the decision to erect a new town hall was made on utilitarian grounds, the corporation seized the opportunity to create a distinguished work of art. In September 1864, the town council declared that it was "prepared to spend any sum which may be reasonably required for the erection of a new Town Hall...equal if not superior to any building in the country."[14]

Both symbolic and economic considerations entered into the choice of the site as well as into the planning of the entire building. Some opted for a site near the infirmary, because they believed that the New Town Hall should stand on the highest land in the city; others preferred the town yard site, a largely uncleared piece of property in the heart of Manchester, part of which was already owned by the corporation. The town councillors opted for the latter because it was less expensive than buying the land surrounding the infirmary and because they wanted to develop the area, which was later named the Albert Square. It seems likely that the Town Hall, like the Albert Memorial, was located in this area because the corporation was anxious to secure "an open space in the centre of the city, which whilst adding materially to its general appearance will improve the sanitary conditions of the District."[15] Their aim was to build an imposing square with impressive architectural works that would at once refurbish the city center and demonstrate Manchester's commitment to artistic excellence.

Examining the backgrounds and expectations of the men who directed the making of the Manchester New Town Hall helps

illuminate the values it expressed and the needs it met. Although many town councillors actively participated in this vast project, the signatures of two men in particular, Abel Heywood and Joseph Thompson, are inscribed in the fabric of the municipal palace.

What is most striking about these individuals is that they were representative middle-class liberals. Abel Heywood, who first proposed the project and served as the chairman of the New Town Hall Committee since its inception, was truly the "architect of his own fortune." Self-help and self-reliance, intelligence and determination, earnestness and piety – these classic virtues of the Victorian middle class informed his life. Born in 1810, the boy who became the mayor of Manchester worked in the warehouse of Thomas Worthington from the time he was nine until he was twenty. A lover of learning, he began his education in his spare time – what little spare time he had – at a Nonconformist's Sunday School and then went on to a mechanics' institute, where he pursued a general plan of "self-culture." Convinced that moving on in the world meant moving out of the warehouse, he did just that and opened a print shop. His business soon flourished, and he became well known as a publisher and a bookseller with a radical bent. He was one of the original members of the town council in 1836, taking a special interest in the Highway, Paving and Sewers Committee, which he chaired for forty-seven years. An enthusiastic Liberal, he served as mayor of Manchester during the cotton famine and then solidified his reputation as a "man of the people" who treated squire and artisan alike. It was said of Abel Heywood that he was, above all, a man of business, "bad at grooming," but with "plenty of go." In this he was a Mancunian to the fingertips.[16]

His junior colleague Joseph Thompson did not have the benefit of the self-made man's disadvantages. His life exemplified the pattern of many Victorian middle-class families: After they had become financially secure, their scions often turned to the world of culture. Born in 1833 to an affluent, tasteful family that had lived in Manchester for generations, he had far more opportunity for self-development than the

impoverished Heywood. Whereas Heywood had to struggle for what little formal instruction he obtained, Joseph Thompson was educated at a noted Nonconformist's boarding school in Amersham and at Owens College, which he later served as its treasurer and chronicled as its historian. Although he was not the architect of his own fortune, he did build up the highly successful cotton manufacturing firm established by his grandfather and carried on by his father. He also followed the family tradition of active participation in local government, serving, like his father before him, as the councillor for the affluent southeastern suburb of Ardwick beginning in 1865. An ardent Liberal and founder of the Reform Club, he served on almost all the committees of the town council until graduating into the "departments of public taste," to which he was best suited temperamentally. A "thorough educationist" known for his piety and learning, he devoted himself both to the arts, as a patron and then as chairman of the Manchester Art Gallery, and to technology, as a leader of the movement for a new ship canal.[17]

That the making of the Manchester Town Hall was directed by middle-class businessmen who were Liberals in politics and Nonconformists in religion has two important ramifications. In the first place, the examples of Abel Heywood and Joseph Thompson suggest that Matthew Arnold, in his *Culture and Anarchy* (1869), did not succeed in seeing things steadily or in seeing them whole. He argued that the middle class, especially in the "great towns" of the provinces, were narrow-minded, materialistic philistines who were insensitive to the state, history, and culture. Yet this portrait fits neither Heywood nor Thompson nor Manchester. They certainly had an "idea of the State," although they were dedicated to local self-government, to the polis, rather than centralized authority. Had Manchester been unaware of the value of government there would have been no need to spend one million pounds on a town hall to accommodate the diverse departments of the municipality. Although it is unlikely that either man adhered to Arnold's rather cloying vision of "sweetness and light," they were both dedicated to elevating the educational and

cultural standards of Manchester. Had their concern with culture been limited, Manchester men never would have sponsored Owens College (1851), the Art Treasures Exhibition (1857), or the founding of the Hallé Orchestra (1858). There was, of course, some truth to Arnold's charges, but to take his word as an accurate sketch of the world of the industrial middle class is both naïve and unwarranted. Second, that Heywood and Thompson were both middle-class liberals involved in the mainstream of Manchester life suggests once again that medievalism was not simply a revolt against industrial capitalism perpetrated by marginal men.

Civic pride inspired the attempt to rehabilitate medieval architecture for the glory of Manchester. When the proposal for a new municipal building was first announced, Joseph Thompson offered his views on the matter in a letter to a local newspaper. "Let the authorities remember," he warned, shortly before he was to join their number, "that the eyes of the country are upon them in this matter and that we shall not be held excusable if we choose a bad site...Manchester has not hitherto had much to boast of architecturally; let us not throw away an opportunity such as we are not likely to have again to do something worthy of the position in this country and the world our busy city holds."[18] Like the other provincials we have met in this study, Thompson was deeply concerned about the image his town had in the eyes of the nation. He hoped that the New Town Hall, like the recently completed Assize Courts, would beautify the squalid appearance of Manchester. And he hoped that a great building would put the town on the cultural map and demonstrate that Manchester had a flair for art as well as for business – as he himself did. Joseph Thompson was, in short, culturally ambitious, and for him as for other Victorians public buildings were, on one level, a form of competition.

Abel Heywood was also concerned with the image of Manchester. "By universal admission," he noted, looking back at the project as an old man, "the Town Hall is a worthy monument of the industrial greatness of Manchester and an outward and visible sign to the world that we are not wholly

given up to Mammon and that the higher culture is not neglected among us."[19] Although doing battle with Mammon
was the duty of every pious Christian, the devils that haunted
Heywood flourished in a specific historical milieu: the Manchester of the early nineteenth century, in which he himself
grew up and prospered under conditions of great difficulty.
His statement implies that for him the making of the New
Town Hall was a means to transform the cultural image as
well as the visual reality of Manchester.

The attempt to fight materialism through historic architecture was not unique to Manchester or, for that matter, confined to medieval styles. Asa Briggs showed that public buildings
in the provinces were the children of a civic pride that was
fortified by the desire to compete with neighboring towns and
with London. They were meant to raise standards of taste and
beautify the townscape of smoky, unattractive industrial centers. This position was articulated by such representatives of
the "cultured classes" as Dr. John Heaton, who played an
important role in the making of the Leeds Town Hall, a Neo-
Renaissance structure designed by Cuthbert Broderick. "If a
noble municipal palace that might fairly vie with some of the
best Town Halls of the Continent were to be erected in the
middle of this hitherto squalid and unbeautiful town," argued
Heaton, "it would become a practical admonition to the popu-
lace of the value of beauty and art, and in course of time men
would live up to it." Like Heywood, Dr. Heaton hoped the
Town Hall would reveal that in "the ardour of mercantile
pursuits the inhabitants of Leeds have not omitted to cultivate the perception of the beautiful and a taste for the fine
arts."[20] Dignity, stateliness, and grandeur were the qualities
that Heaton and his kindred sought in their public architecture; these were the qualities that they found in the various
styles of the Western past.

The New Town Hall should also be seen in the broad context of the campaign to make Manchester a worthy city. The
problem in Manchester, as in comparable industrial centers,
was how to transform an urban environment whose conditions were often disgraceful. Even the middle-class elite, the

sponsors and beneficiaries of progress, seem to have had little liking for certain aspects of city life. That is why it was conventional for businessmen and professionals to move to suburbs like Victoria Park or, less frequently, to country homes in places like Cheshire. The result of their migrations was to leave the city center to the poorest elements of the community, the victims of industrialization. The environs of what later became the Albert Square were notorious for unsanitary conditions, squalid housing, high death rates, and the presence of a "highly criminal element." The erection of the New Town Hall was part of a general program to rehabilitate the city. Piecemeal and inadequate as this program was, still it included the reconditioning of working-class housing, the creation of parks and other "open spaces" like the Albert Square designed to relieve the congestion of the inner city, and the construction of an extensive drainage and sewage system and of gasworks.[21]

There were three main reasons why it was particularly pressing to rehabilitate the city center of Manchester during the 1860s and 1870s when the New Town Hall was planned and built. First, during this period the central authorities in London decided that their local counterparts in the great cities of England were either unwilling to deal with the enormous social problems they faced, or incapable of doing so. This charge was somewhat unfair, as Manchester and Liverpool had led the fight to enact parliamentary legislation to deal with urban problems. Yet the central authorities compelled them to take action through legislative measures like the Artisan and Labourers' Dwellings Act (1868), which called for slum clearance and consequent relocation of displaced persons in the same district. Second, as the tram system expanded, suburban living became a practical, appealing alternative for the working class, who, like the middle classes before them, deserted the city center in increasing numbers. The threat of population decline – a threat realized between 1871 and 1881 – disturbed the corporation for economic, not sentimental, reasons. The outward drift of the population meant a loss of revenue that was critically important because of the obligation to improve

the conditions of the city. Finally, as industry and population drifted out of Manchester proper, the inner core became a commercial center for a twenty-mile radius. It was, therefore, particularly important for it to be as attractive as possible, to lure people back to the city from the suburbs.[22]

The construction of the Town Hall was the most striking, significant part of the rehabilitation of Manchester. It symbolized the corporation's attempt to make Manchester a "provincial metropolis" by extending the scope and power of local government and by amalgamating surrounding townships. To understand the architectural form of the building and the needs it served, it is necessary to examine how and why Alfred Waterhouse obtained the commission to design the Neo-Gothic municipal palace.

Although civic pride was a powerful motive in the making of the Manchester Town Hall, the city fathers bypassed local experts and turned to London's community of professional architects to formulate their taste. The municipal palace was meant to rival the architecture of the capital, but insecurity made the metropolitan seal of approval a virtual necessity. Here the provincial search for cultural respectability coincided with the attempt of professional architects to establish their hegemony as the sole proprietors of taste and beauty.

The town council decided that the commission for the building should be determined by a formal competition. If this practice was no more the invention of Mancunians than of any Victorians — it throve, for example, in Renaissance Florence — it was particularly appropriate for a culture that prized free traffic in business as in art and was, moreover, trying to create new aesthetic norms. Especially because recent competitions, such as that for the new Government Offices, Whitehall, seemed scandalously unfair to many observers, not to mention the feelings of the unsuccessful participants, the town council was intent on ensuring that their contest was free from jobbery and favoritism. The decision-making process was to consist of two stages: an initial evaluation, from which not

more than twelve or less than six architects would be invited to revise sketches, and a final judgment.[23] The council stated their clear preference for Gothic, but they neither explained their rationale nor prohibited the use of other styles.[24] The *Builder* – which acerbically noted that perhaps in two hundred years England might have a rational architectural competition system – criticized the Mancunian plan on the grounds that it was time consuming and costly for architects. But it approved of the decision to pay the finalists generously and to use professional assessors to judge the competition.[25]

The great drama that pervades the competition for the Palace of Westminster and the Royal Law Courts is not to be found in the story of the Manchester New Town Hall. Although this may disappoint those who relish exciting plots, no doubt most contemporary architects were pleased by the relatively businesslike regularity and efficiency of the contest, especially as these were rarities in the mid-Victorian building world. On 1 July 1867 the town clerk, Joseph Heron, had in his possession 137 designs, all of which were limited to three elevations and two plans. Appointing George Godwin, the estimable editor of the *Builder*, as judge for the first round was a clever way to silence the criticisms of his journal. He selected eleven designs by nine architects, one of whom was disqualified for an infringement of the rules. William Lee, John Oldrid Scott, Edward Salomons, Speakman and Charlesworth, Thomas Worthington, Alfred Waterhouse, T. H. Wyatt, and Cuthbert Broderick were asked to submit further, more detailed, more polished designs. On 14 February 1867 two new judges, also eminent members of the London architectural establishment, the classicist Professor T. L. Donaldson and the Goth George Edmund Street, received these new sketches.

Valentine's Day 1867 proved to be a triumph for the admirers of medieval architecture, as all but two of the final designs were in the Neo-Gothic style. One of the men who opted for the Italian classic style, T. H. Wyatt, argued that it was far more suitable to the "atmosphere of Manchester" and to modern functional demands than either Gothic or Elizabethan. He added that as Manchester already possessed in the

Assize Courts a distinguished Gothic edifice, there was no need to build another, especially as it might clash with Waterhouse's structure.[26] The other competitors did not indulge in such self-serving logic. Their explanations of their designs are of special interest, because they reveal how medieval architecture provided a contemporary aesthetic ideal. Cuthbert Broderick, who called himself "Arnolfo di Lopo" – all the contestants assumed pseudonyms to ensure anonymity and hence impartiality – took as his model the "most magnificent and beautiful Town Hall in existence, Ypres, built in the thirteenth century, the golden age of Gothic architecture," which saw "the most glorious buildings that ever existed."[27] So too did J. O. Scott, "Sperandum," who praised the town halls of Flemish and German manufacturing cities. He was quick to add that Gothic was also "adaptable to the requirements, materials and modes of construction belonging to our present day."[28] The point here is that even those who idealized the Middle Ages as an aesthetic golden age realized that Gothic could be used to set contemporary taste only if it was demonstrably practical.

This was borne out by the results of the competition. The judges placed Speakman and Charlesworth first for the excellence of the elevation and gave J. O. Scott second place, Thomas Worthington third, and Alfred Waterhouse fourth. But in other crucial matters, such as general arrangement and convenience, simplicity of plan, and facilities of access, light, and ventilation, they found Waterhouse clearly superior to his competitors.[29] It should surprise no one that in Manchester utility prevailed: Waterhouse was declared the winner of the competition. Quite unconsciously the judges substantiated Léon Faucher's quip: "Everything is measured in its results by the standard of utility; and if THE BEAUTIFUL, THE GREAT AND THE NOBLE, ever take root in Manchester, they will be developed in accordance with this standard."[30]

The town councillors did not hesitate to ask for a second report explaining the rationale for the decision, which they duly received, but they happily accepted the outcome. After all, Alfred Waterhouse, the architect of the much-acclaimed

Manchester Assize Courts, was no stranger to them. This was especially true for Joseph Thompson, who enjoyed a friendship with the architect and kept in touch with him throughout the competition. Initially, Waterhouse was so preoccupied with his design for the Royal Law Courts competition – he had moved from his Manchester home, Balcombe House, to London in order to devote himself fully to the task – that he was unable to give close attention to the first set of Manchester New Town Hall sketches. "But," he wrote to Thompson, who had seen his design before the proceedings began and leniently criticized it, "I hope to have the chance of showing you better things by being one of the selected few."[31] Delighted as he was by his ultimate victory, Waterhouse was still very annoyed by the handling of the competition: He was resentful that the faults of his design were publicized, whereas those of his competitors were not. He did, however, make a point of thanking Thompson for "turning the tide of public opinion in my favor," an intriguing hint as to the cotton merchant's role that was not further elucidated.[32]

Alfred Waterhouse's broad significance for our story is that in his person he bridged the gap between professionalism and provincialism and in his art he married the practical and the picturesque. His social background and experience equipped him to understand the style of life and outlook, the needs and aspirations, of his clients. Like them, he was a native of Lancashire, born in Aigburth, on the outskirts of Liverpool, in 1830. Brought up almost exclusively in Quaker circles until he went up to Cambridge at eighteen, he could well understand Abel Heywood's fear of Mammon and his resolve to fight materialism through art. Alfred Waterhouse can be seen as a mirror image of Joseph Thompson, who was almost his exact contemporary: The one an artist with the acute pragmatism of a businessman and the other a businessman deeply interested and involved in the arts. The architect's path to artistic achievement, like that of Manchester itself, was not an easy one. It was only with difficulty that he persuaded his pious parents to allow him to pursue his artistic bent. As pragmatic Quakers they revered the Inner Light, but they also

wanted to know how it was going to be fueled. Hence, they quickly vetoed the prospect of a career in painting or sculpture and instead urged their son to take up architecture, a more businesslike, secure, and respectable art that was undergoing professionalization in the first years of Victoria's reign.

By virtue of his professional training and experience, Waterhouse was at ease in Manchester and London. He first acquired his intimate knowledge of Manchester when he apprenticed himself to a rather undistinguished local architect, Richard Lane, in 1847. It was in Manchester that he opened his first office, built his first buildings, such as the Binyon and Fryer Warehouse (1855), and obtained the commission for the Manchester Assize Courts (1859), which virtually assured him of future financial success and artistic renown. He moved to London in 1865, but he never lost touch with his old contacts in Manchester. More than any other provincial architect his buildings achieved a national celebrity, which his colleagues at the Royal Institute of British Architects recognized when they awarded him their gold medal (1878) and elected him president of their organization (1888–91). His aesthetic orientation also suited him for the Manchester Town Hall commission. His practice covered an astonishing range of building types, including churches, colleges, country homes, and museums, but he was best known and most skilled as a civic and commercial architect. Although he was, from the first, a Gothic architectural artist, his was a self-consciously modern style that gave equal attention to functional and picturesque considerations.[33]

What the leaders of taste thought praiseworthy in Neo-Gothic architecture is revealed by the critical response to the New Town Hall designs. After the results of the competition were announced, an exhibition was held in order to display the sketches to the public and professional communities. The *Manchester Guardian* criticized Cuthbert Broderick's version of thirteenth-century Gothic for being too exact a copy, a lifeless reproduction that betrayed a "lack of the originating power which every architect of our Victorian age must at least in some measure possess."[34] The charge that the design showed

151

Broderick to be out of sympathy with medieval architecture was particularly ironic on two counts: Although he was best known as the architect of the Neo-Renaissance Leeds Town Hall, he had begun his career as a devoted Goth; and it was he who praised the thirteenth century as an aesthetic golden age in the explanation of his design quoted earlier. This brings us to the first important aesthetic criterion at work here: Historic models were to serve as points of departure, not destinations. Artistic originality was, as is well known, far more important by the 1860s than was archeological accuracy. The evaluation of T. H. Wyatt's rationale for his classic design is equally telling. The editors did not accept the idea that it was far better suited to the "atmosphere of Manchester" than was the Gothic style. Not only had recent building proved to their satisfaction that Gothic could be a source of contemporary aesthetic standards because of its functionality, but its Christian roots and associations made it far preferable to other modes of expression.[35]

What did the *Manchester Guardian* believe was suitable for the atmosphere of "Cottonopolis"? Like the professional jury, the provincial leaders of taste favored Alfred Waterhouse. They argued that his design represented an excellent solution to the practical problems posed by the irregularity of the site. They were particularly impressed by Waterhouse's preference for the practical over the aesthetic, the real over the ideal. Indeed, their overstatement of this aspect of his work betrays the weight utilitarian considerations had in their architectural values. Yet they sought a higher functionalism: Utility had to be beautified to be acceptable. They faulted Waterhouse's design for the "lack of dignity" in the main entrance but praised it for the richness of the apartments and especially for the serenity and simplicity of his "grand architectural display." The newspaper also maintained that Waterhouse's New Town Hall would surely take its place among the Palace of Westminster, the Law Courts, and the National Gallery, adding an "architectural adornment to our somewhat prosaic town, which may be honorable to us, and hold an important place in the national architecture of Great Britain."[36] Not only Joseph Thomp-

son harbored cultural and aesthetic ambitions; not only Abel Heywood hoped to show that Manchester was not entirely given up to Mammon.

These evaluations of the New Town Hall designs are most significant in that they reveal that the *Manchester Guardian*, one of liberal England's most important organs, accepted the taste defined by the mid-Victorian architectural community. Nowhere is this better highlighted than in their preference for Gothic. The newspaper, which did so much to shape Mancunian political and cultural ideals, interpreted the victory of Waterhouse's design as yet another proof that "our national architecture is again to return to that great school of art whose principles were so truthfully and wonderfully expounded by its revival champion, the late A. W. Pugin."[37] That the principles of Pugin, one of the most formidable critics of the industrial, capitalist, Protestant world that Manchester epitomized, appealed to its leaders is an irony well worth disentangling.

There are many ways to explain the architectural form of Neo-Gothic buildings like the Manchester New Town Hall. One can argue that the council was influenced by the architecture of the Houses of Parliament and recent civic buildings in the north as well as by the local precedent of the Assize Courts. Although this is true enough, the argument that their choice was conventional cannot explain the cultural logic of this convention, for it is valid only if we bear in mind that conventions depend upon the understanding and acceptance of a set of shared meanings and signs in a particular social community. It is then necessary to attend to the specific historical associations that Gothic carried for Victorians.

It is possible to argue that the taste for Gothic in middle-class industrial centers was an attempt to imitate an aristocratic style and a symptom of an aristocratic nostalgia for an idyllic rural past. One writer has put forth this thesis using the Bradford Wool Exchange as a case in point.[38] Yet even a brief glance at the fascinating iconography of this building shows how misleading this argument is. The medallions on

its exterior depict not feudal lords but textile manufacturers such as Richard Arkwright and Sir Titus Salt as well as inventors and engineers such as James Watt and George Stephenson. Its interior contains a sculptural series concerning the legends of Bishop Blaize, the medieval patron saint of the wool trade, whose festival was celebrated in Bradford throughout the nineteenth century. Like Edward Collinson's and John James's histories of the wool trade, the imagery of the Bradford Wool Exchange represents the historic roots and contemporary achievements of commerce and industry. In so doing, it highlighted their romance and demonstrated their respectability.

To understand the significance of the popularity of Gothic architecture in the industrial north it is necessary to distinguish forms and functions. There was traffic in significant symbols between different classes and regions in Victorian society, but this is not to say that the significance of the forms did not change en route. Much as the image of the cross in paintings by Titian, Caspar David Friedrich, and Mark Rothko might assume very different functions in light of the total canvas, so also could the meaning of Neo-Gothic architecture vary considerably according to its settings and makers.

It is fruitful to interpret the social and cultural meanings of the pervasive use of the Neo-Gothic style in Manchester from the 1860s to the 1890s in light of the functions it served. Its most striking impact was to transform the visual identity of the "shock city of the industrial revolution." The picturesque qualities of Gothic architecture – roughness, intricacy, variety, movement, adornment, asymmetry – provided a superb counterpoint to a prosaic townscape in which utility had destroyed nature. By creating the illusion of naturalness, Gothic architecture lent the scenic beauty of the countryside to the urban environment. The rehabilitation of medieval architectural forms furnished Victorians with an indispensable means to refurbish their city centers as well as their garden suburbs according to the ideal of *rus in urbe*. This was particularly important in Manchester because of the dismal conditions of the inner city.

The symbolic meanings of Gothic architecture also made it an appropriate medium for expressing the civic style and aspi-

rations of Manchester. Its historical associations with the affluent medieval Italian, Flemish, and German cities governed by an elite of merchants who had liberated themselves from the feudal aristocracy naturally appealed to middle-class liberals, who could hardly identify with the baronial or ecclesiastical associations of Gothic. This point was not lost on Benjamin Disraeli, whose vigorous imagination and no less vigorous urge to flatter helped him half perceive and half create the romance of industry. In 1843, in a speech delivered, appropriately enough, at the Free Trade Hall in Manchester, he exhorted his audience to follow the historical ideal of the merchant princes of the Middle Ages, who had used their wealth to patronize the arts and to cultivate their sensibilities and intellects.[39] Victorians also hailed medieval cities for their contributions to the cause of local self-government. In 1874, Joseph Chamberlain insisted upon the medieval roots of his civic gospel in a speech he gave at the ceremony for the laying of the cornerstone of Birmingham's Council House.

> Let me remind you that those old communities from whom we derive the model of our municipal institutions were never behind-hand in the discharge of this duty. We find in the old cities of the Continent – of Belgium, and Germany, and Italy – the free and independent burghers of the Middle Ages have left behind them magnificent palaces and civic buildings – testimonies to their power and public spirit and munificence, memorials of the time when those communities maintained the liberties and protected the lives of the people against the oppression, and the tyranny, and the rapacity of their rulers.[40]

Political radicals as well as reactionaries traced the genealogies of their ideal and programs back to medieval forms.

The proliferation of Gothic forms shaped the civic image no less than the visual reality of Manchester: "Manchester," said the local architect Thomas Worthington, a talented practitioner and leading proponent of the Italian Gothic style, "is acquiring a reputation of a town of some architectural character; it

is the inland metropolis of the North – the Florence, if I may so describe it, of the nineteenth century; it has developed a style of architecture which we may largely call our own and in which we may take a not unnatural pride."[41] Such distinguished buildings as Alfred Waterhouse's New Town Hall tended to efface the image of Manchester as the "shock city of the industrial revolution." It demonstrated that if Manchester men had ever been philistine materialists given up to Mammon, those days were gone. It showed that the present leaders of the city were men of taste and sensibility, keenly aware of the importance of aesthetic achievement and so mindful of the common good that they spared no expense in erecting their municipal palace. It justified Manchester's claim to be the "inland metropolis of the north" that could rival London in art as well as in business.

Seen in the context of its historical associations, it is clear that the use of the Gothic style in Manchester was not simply an attempt to mimic the aristocracy. Rather, it defined the cultural style of Manchester as a commercial metropolis dedicated to aesthetic achievement and municipal dignity, and it celebrated, in effect, the revival of the medieval commune. That the Town Hall was meant to connect Manchester with the glorious achievements of the burgher past is also implied by the outcome of the debate over what it should be called. The self-conscious rejection of the name "City Hall" is particularly interesting, because Manchester had only earned that prestigious title in 1853.[42] Yet, "Gemeinschaft" triumphed over "Gesellschaft," and the name "Town Hall," with its resonances of communal harmony and intimacy, was adopted.

By designing their Town Hall in the Gothic style, the political leaders of Manchester engineered a cultural coup. They appropriated and assimilated the art form that had largely been the cultural property of aristocratic, conservative, rural England to legitimize, glorify, and beautify middle-class, progressive, urban England. Just as the leaders of Manchester proclaimed their hegemony over medieval architecture to fashion a civic style, so too did they preempt the figures and myths of their historic inheritance to define idealized cultural and

social values. To examine how this was done we must now turn to the elaborate iconography of the municipal palace.

The celebration of provincial liberalism

The iconography of the Manchester Town Hall was planned by Alfred Waterhouse and Joseph Thompson in conjunction with the New Town Hall Committee. Between 1867 and 1877, as the building was constructed, and to a lesser extent from 1878 to 1893, when the remainder of the decorative program was executed, Waterhouse and Thompson corresponded and met regularly to discuss the problems involved in creating a huge, complicated building. Their letters furnish glimpses of them doing historical research to determine which individuals and events from the civic past should be depicted in the New Town Hall. They chose subjects that marked out a particular period in Manchester's history and insisted on historical authenticity in the costumes of the statues. Their program focused on "whatever identified itself with the city" and honored those worthies who had been benefactors of Manchester.[43] The basic strategy of the iconography was outlined in one of Waterhouse's letters. Explaining the rationale of his proposed decorations for the Reception Room in 1876, he wrote that he was "anxious to get the arms of some of the distinguished families of the neighbourhood such as would be likely *to do us some credit.*"[44] Waterhouse underlined the final phrase, first, because of its mercantile overtones; second, because the use of "us" indicates his close identification with the town and its ruling elite. The entire statement is most interesting, however, because it suggests that Waterhouse attempted to preempt traditional symbols, such as heraldry and family crests, to legitimize and glorify historic and contemporary Manchester.

The speeches delivered at the opening ceremonies of the Town Hall in September 1877 illuminate the concerns that the iconography of the building symbolized. The leaders of Manchester were concerned with the future of local self-

government, one of English Liberalism's most cherished ideals. "We further trust," said the town clerk, Joseph Heron, "that the principles of local self-government consecrated by glorious traditions and embodied in our Charter and Municipal Acts, may long be duly recognized and supported, and may ever escape all centralizing influences, which are destructive alike of civil liberty and independence."[45] Another major concern was the status of free trade and the manufacturing system, on which the prosperity of Manchester depended. John Bright told his former constituents that "although the past and the present are so brilliant, I cannot help thinking that we are all conscious of the fact that the future is not without anxiety, and even I may say that the present is not without its clouds."[46] One of these clouds was the image of Manchester as a citadel of philistine materialism. In his speech, Dr. Fraser, the bishop of Manchester, criticized "those carpings which dainty and witty gentlemen leading a pleasant club life in London indulged in at the expense of Manchester when they told them what a vulgar set of people they were, overspreading the land with their low commercial habits and sentiments."[47] The language of his statement indicates that cultural stereotypes were not the exclusive preserve of the "dainty and witty gentlemen of London."

These preoccupations must be examined in the context of the problems faced by Manchester and comparable cities in the 1870s. One of the major themes of this period was the acrimonious struggle between the national and the municipal governments over the boundaries of their respective rights and responsibilities. The former called for the centralization of policy and administration because the latter had done all too little to improve the conditions of urban life. The local authorities of Manchester, whose social consciences had been kindled, if not inflamed, by the miseries caused by the cotton famine and then by the disclosures of the horrible sanitary, health, and housing conditions of the slums, agreed that public action was called for. Yet they objected to the charge that their previous efforts were as lackadaisical as they were ineffective and to the idea that they would do little or nothing

without coercion. And they also objected, with some justification, to the increase in their social obligations just as their political power was diminished. The Local Government Board Act (1871), for instance, made it difficult for them to propose a bill to Parliament. It required an absolute majority of the council and the prior approval of the representatives of the national authorities and the Local Government Board. Municipal leaders did all they could to stop what they saw as intolerable interference in, and subversion of, the principle of local self-government. They believed that the problems at hand were best approached through centralization at the local level: the consolidation of existing administrative machinery and the expansion of local statutory powers.[48] Thus, when the Lord Chief Justice proposed a toast to "The Prosperity of the Municipal Corporations of the United Kingdom" at the banquet following the opening of the New Town Hall, we can presume that both the councillors and their constituents drank with relish and resentment.[49]

Manchester was not free from the "chill in the air" that G. M. Young sensed in the atmosphere of late-Victorian England. The hegemony of political Liberalism was threatened by the newly enfranchised sections of the working class, whose political allegiance was at least partly unpredictable. It was far more difficult in Manchester than in Birmingham to create an alliance between the middle class and the working class, because Manchester lacked a tradition of political cooperation between the two groups. Birmingham, not Manchester, became the leading late-Victorian city, a shift symbolized by Richard Cobden's defeat in 1857 and Bright's move to Birmingham. Not the least of the difficulties of the 1870s were economic. The great boom of the high-Victorian years evaporated with the financial crash of 1873, the fall in interest rates and commodity prices, and the increase in foreign competition. There were also more general changes evident by the 1870s. By this time the golden age of textile manufacturing and merchandising was decidedly over as the steel and engineering industries assumed new importance. Gone too was the heyday of the self-made men of the early-industrial era,

the energetic, resourceful, ambitious entrepreneurs who contributed so much to the fame, and notoriety, of Manchester. The passage of limited liability laws, the routinization of commercial and industrial life, the establishment of the new unionism – these developments signaled fundamental shifts in the world of work.[50] All this is not to say that Manchester was no longer prosperous and powerful, but only to emphasize that it was losing the dominant role it possessed in the first half of the nineteenth century. Hence, John Bright's fear of decline was well warranted.

There was also good reason for Dr. Fraser's sensitivity about the image of Manchester. Matthew Arnold's *Culture and Anarchy* was the most powerful assault on Manchester. He criticized the world of "our Liberal friends" on numerous grounds: its bondage to machinery, its overestimation of the value of the franchise, its dedication to "doing as one likes" and the consequent neglect of the "social question," and, finally, for its philistine disregard for culture.[51] Not unlike the proponents of political centralization who attacked local self-government, Arnold condemned provincialism as narrow-minded, incomplete, and vulgar.

It is in the context of these challenges that the iconography of the Town Hall must be understood. The municipal palace exemplifies the manufacture of tradition and the display of its wares; it celebrated the achievements of provincial liberalism through historical imagery. The subjects of all the painting and sculpture of the building were drawn from the history of Manchester and its region, with the exception of statues of the patron saint of England, St. George, and of several angels. These images demonstrated persuasively that Manchester, far from being an upstart town without roots, was in fact a "place of high antiquity," with traditions as rich and praiseworthy as those of towns like York and Winchester, Oxford and Hastings.[52] Picturing the past was particularly important because despite the town's age, it possessed few historical survivals. Its chief relics, the medieval Baron's Hall and Cathedral as well as a fragment of the Roman Wall, were too insignificant to satisfy even the hungry gaze of eager tourists. Although its preoccupation with the historic inheritance of Manchester gives the Town Hall the air of a bourgeois museum, it would be wrong to see it merely as a swansong in stone. Memory was recruited in the service of contemporary aims. The iconography provided a striking guide to, and visual archive of, the history of the city. By portraying the past achievements of local worthies, it reflected and revivified provincial self-consciousness and pride, and provided animating ideals for Mancunians. It was especially important to define the identity of Manchester as the city grew and its liberal ideals were undermined by changing social realities. "It stands visibly reminding every citizen of Manchester," commented the *Manchester Guardian,* "of the labour and responsibilities of the community to which he belongs, appealing to men of every rank and station each in his way to unite in helping forward the common interest of all."[53] Images from the local past provided overarching myths and symbols that were acceptable to most groups.

The basic thrust of the political imagery was to sketch the roots and growth of such treasured contemporary ideals and forms as municipal freedom and parliamentary rights. Its crucial function was to legitimize the threatened power of local self-government by displaying the ancient origins of Manchester's right to rule itself. To this end, the exterior of the building houses statues of Thomas de Gresley, the lord of Manchester who granted the Charter of 1301, which made it a free borough; King Henry III and Queen Elizabeth I, both of whom also granted charters that enlarged the scope of local self-government; and General Worsley of Platt, the friend of Cromwell who became Manchester's first parliamentary representative. Although the iconography stressed the historical dimension of municipal life, the nineteenth century was not neglected. The reform of local and national government is symbolized by the coats of arms of the town's last boroughreeve, followed by those of its Victorian mayors and first representative to the post–1832 Parliament.

161

The economic imagery celebrated another central tenet of the Liberal creed, the belief in free trade, and highlighted the romance of industry. The leitmotivs depicted on its floors and ceilings, its stained glass and stonework, its exterior and interior represent the making of "Cottonopolis." The emblems of the cotton plant and shuttle represent how Manchester men used technology to create a product that was, as A.J.P. Taylor pointed out, a blessing to mankind in addition to being a boon for business. The image of the bee embodied the belief in the virtue of work and industriousness, and that of the ship represents the international trade that made Manchester far more than just another English provincial town. Throughout the building these themes are elaborated. A statue of King Edward III, who with his wife, Queen Philippa, induced the Flemings to come to England, refers to a local myth that held this act to be the foundation of Manchester's textile industries. So too do the two medallions of the exterior, which illustrate the "old style of spinning and weaving," thus displaying the antiquity of commerce and manufacturing. That Manchester's merchants had long been honorable, munificent men devoted to far more than merely "getting on" is symbolized by a statue of Humphrey Chetham, the Tudor merchant who endowed the boys' school that still bears his name. Again, the world of the nineteenth century received its due: The statues of John Bright and Charles Villiers, Liberal heroes of the fight for free trade and foes of aristocratic privilege, occupy places of honor in the building. And the coats of arms of numerous entrepreneurs, including the Duke of Bridgewater, who sponsored the local canal that facilitated trade; and those of inventors, like James Watt, who devised the steam engine, were sculpted on the facade of the municipal palace. The magnificent ceiling of the Great Hall is decorated not with the arms of knights and nobles but with large panels that depict the characteristic symbols of the wide range of nations and cities with which Manchester traded – from America to Egypt, from Liverpool to Vienna. Like the ships, these panels highlight Manchester's cosmopolitan character and international associations, demonstrating that Arnold's equation of provincialism with insu-

larity was, in point of fact, false. Once again it must be stressed that these commercial and industrial realities were represented through the traditional medium of heraldry and the like, presumably for legitimacy.

There are also two minor iconographical patterns. The first sketches the religious history of Manchester to highlight its devotion to Christianity. The transformation of religious life is represented by statues of Thomas de la Warre, the fourteenth-century founder of the Collegiate Church, and John Bradford, the Protestant martyr of the age of Queen Mary, as well as by the heraldic bearings of a host of nineteenth-century churchmen, both Dissenters and Anglicans. The second pattern locates Manchester in its region by depicting the rose, the symbol of the Duchy of Lancashire, throughout the building. A similar message is conveyed by shields emblazoned with the arms of Manchester and those of surrounding towns that depended on it, such as Salford, Rochdale, Bolton, Preston, Oldham, Stockport, Ashton-under-Lyme, and Stalybridge. All these images symbolized Manchester's claim to be a provincial capital, the "inland metropolis of the North."

The murals in the Great Hall of the New Town Hall, which were painted between 1878 and 1893, also exemplify the creation of a civic tradition. Controversy surrounded them from the first, when the choice of artist proved problematic. Local painters and their supporters were outraged by the prospect of the commission being granted to foreign artists, the Belgian painters Jan Swerts and Godfried Guffens, who were known for their skill and experience in fresco technique. They argued that English artists were capable of carrying out even the most exacting task. Bowing to public pressure, the city fathers granted the commission jointly to Manchester painter Frederic Shields, who eventually withdrew from the agreement before completing a single canvas, and his close friend, Ford Madox Brown, the socially radical mentor of the Pre-Raphaelite brotherhood who had distinguished himself in both historical and contemporary painting and was already popular in Manchester.[54]

The next question was What subjects should the murals portray? The *British Architect,* a professional journal published

163

in Manchester, was certain as to the proper course of action. It contended that the murals were an excellent opportunity for Manchester to make a major aesthetic contribution to the nation. Whereas the friezes of classical Egypt and Greece depicted scenes from contemporary life, Victorian England was obsessed with producing "pseudo-classical or mediaeval misrepresentations."[55] Manchester, as a city full of the "associations and poetry of modern life," should picture the wonders of the industrial world rather than give evidence on what the nineteenth century thought of the archaic past. "Have we so little faith in ourselves...so little pride in our life and work," asked the writer, "that we are ashamed to let the world of a thousand years hence know what manner of men we are?"[56] Like Baudelaire and Manet, the *British Architect* believed that it was necessary to be of one's own time.

The city fathers, however, did not accept this interpretation of modernity. They proved themselves to be of their own time precisely by their fascination with the past and their desire to use it to inform the present. Several years before actual work on the murals began, Joseph Thompson, as chairman of the Decorations Subcommittee, drew up a list of approximately two hundred and fifty subjects: It embraced the "purely historical" (by which he presumably meant political events), the "social, industrial and scientific phases of history," "scenes of a festive and social nature," and incidents illustrative of local manners and customs, arts and sciences.[57] It was from this original list that Brown, with the help of Shields, selected those subjects he thought "would paint well," those he deemed most appropriate to "instruct the people," and those he himself had long looked forward to painting.[58] At Thompson's suggestion, Brown, who was trained in the "artist-antiquarian" tradition, did considerable historical research in the British Museum Reading Room to immerse himself in the historic dress and scenery he would recreate in the murals.[59]

The rationale of the murals can be clarified by examining an acrimonious controversy that took place in the autumn of 1878. William Axon, the friend and biographer of Cobden, read an unauthorized list of the proposed subjects for the mu-

rals in the *Athenaeum*. Axon, who later wrote *The Annals of Manchester* (1886), judged the proposals by the "double test of relevancy and accuracy."[60] He found them sadly wanting in both respects and reported his complaints to his long-time friend Abel Heywood in a detailed letter. The flaws of two of the contemplated subjects were characteristic of the errors that Axon objected to throughout. "The Roman General Agricola Builds a Fort at Mancenion, A.D. 80" was unacceptable to him because the evidence for Agricola's very presence in Manchester was purely conjectural. Although the trial of Wycliff was undoubtedly an important event, it had no place in a series designed to depict the "rise and progress of Manchester," because Yorkshireman Wycliff had little do to with the Lancashire capital.[61]

Both Thompson and Brown were infuriated by Axon's letter. The cotton merchant did not "hesitate to say that Mr. Axon's strictures are more querulous than conclusive...the carping complaints of a literary critic."[62] The painter agreed that the "bulk of the objections raised were captious and carping and indicative more of spare time on hand than of experience of art."[63] Thompson proved himself to be Axon's peer in erudition, if not in pedantry, in a long letter to the New Town Hall Committee, in which he rebutted the majority of the charges point by point, admitting errors where he found them and expressing his own reservations where he had them. He defended the Roman subject, for instance, by saying that his aim was "to show the people that Castlefield was once a Roman fort, occupied by a Roman general and his troops." He hoped to sharpen the local sense of place by picturing the roots of Manchester, but he had no "intention of giving a photographic portrait of Caius Agricola."[64] Whereas Axon's attitude to the past was unequivocally literal, Thompson's was colored by his civic pride and desire to capture the "spirit of events" and Brown's by his conviction that painting should be "typical" rather than "documentary," designed to "arouse our sympathy for certain great ideas and beautiful phases of nature."[65]

What subjects did the New Town Hall Committee finally authorize? Although Brown himself substituted a painting of

John Dalton for one of the Jacobite Rebellion of 1745 because the former was more directly pertinent to the history of Manchester, Axon's strictures ultimately had little effect on the shape the series assumed. The following list details the position of the murals in the Great Hall and the respective dates of their completion.

1. "The Romans Building a Fort at Mancenion, A.D. 80" (1880)
2. "The Baptism of Edwin" (1879)
3. "The Expulsion of the Danes from Manchester" (1881)
4. "The Establishment of Flemish Weavers in Manchester, A.D. 1363" (1880)
5. "The Trial of Wickliffe" (1886)
6. "The Proclamation Regarding Weights and Measures, A.D. 1556" (1884)
7. "Crabtree Watching the Transit of Venus, A.D. 1639" (1883)
8. "Chetham's Life Dream, A.D. 1640" (1886)
9. "Bradshaw's Defense of Manchester, A.D. 1642" (1893)
10. "John Kay: Inventor of the Fly Shuttle, A.D. 1753" (1890)
11. "The Opening of the Bridgewater Canal, A.D. 1761" (1892)
12. "Dalton Collecting Marsh Fire Gas" (1887)

To ensure their longevity, Brown painted the first seven murals directly on the walls, using a modified Gambier Parry process. But when failing health forced him to return to London, he completed the work in his studio.

The Great Hall murals articulated a civic tradition through the commemoration of heroic scenes from the recent and distant past. Although the murals concentrated on important events in the local past, the subjects represented were, for the most part, directly relevant to the general history of England. Events like the invention of the fly shuttle, for instance, had

THE ESTABLISHMENT OF FLEMISH WEAVERS IN MANCHESTER · A·D · 1363 · № 2

"The Establishment of Flemish Weavers in Manchester." (By permission of the Manchester Public Library.)

indisputably national ramifications. Like the *Historic Towns* series, the murals stressed the connections between provincial and national history to highlight the contribution Manchester made to the making of England, and they tendentiously appropriated individuals and events with little relation to local history in order to bolster the town's contemporary prestige. One such instance was the inclusion in the murals of John Wycliff, whose only link to Manchester was that his patron, John of Gaunt, was the Duke of Lancashire.

The attitudes and activities idealized in the murals demonstrate that the social strains of industrial society gave new meaning and relevance to premodern social forms and standards. The ideal of craftsmanship is embodied in "The Establishment of the Flemish Weavers in Manchester, A.D. 1363." Brown depicted an idyllic scene in which Queen Philippa and her ladies-in-waiting, just returned from maying, look on as

THE PROCLAMATION REGARDING WEIGHTS AND MEASURES · A·D·1556 ❖ No.

"The Proclamation Regarding Weights and Measures." (By permission of the Manchester Public Library.)

the skilled weavers attend to their work. "The Proclamation Regarding Weights and Measures, A.D. 1556," symbolizes the institutionalization of the just price, which guaranteed the quality and quantity of produce. And the belief in reciprocal duty and communal responsibility are represented in a painting of "Chetham's Life Dream, A.D. 1640," which visualizes the cloth merchant's realization of his plan to found a school for orphaned boys.

Yet the main thrust of the murals was to define a tradition that was unmistakably liberal and to celebrate the values of progressive civilization by clothing them in historical dress. Brown's paintings exemplify the search for roots that was fundamental to the Victorian discovery and exploration of familial, provincial, and national histories. The heretic John Wycliff retained his place in the series despite his vague connection to

168

Manchester because Brown saw him as the "Morning Star of the Reformation," a medieval ancestor of the liberal Protestant ethos so fundamental to modern Mancunian life.[66] And even though there was considerable evidence that textile manufacturing existed in Manchester long before the coming of the Flemings, the scene that celebrated medieval craftsmanship also countered the notion that the cotton and wool trades were the preserve of "arrivistes." "Cottonopolis" could, and did, boast of a long pedigree. "The Proclamation Regarding Weights and Measures, A.D. 1556" reveals that the passion for "getting on" was moderated by reverence for commercial integrity and honor. The civic-minded generosity of the middle class was highlighted in Brown's painting of Humphrey Chetham's foundation of a school for boys. The artist explained that Chetham was a "precursor in the seventeenth century of those schemes, educational and philanthropic, which so prominently distinguish the nineteenth."[67] This panel of the relentlessly didactic series also had a point to make: to improve the public image

169

CRABTREE WATCHING THE TRANSIT OF VENUS · A·D·1639 · No 7

"Crabtree Watching the Transit of Venus." (By permission of the Manchester Public Library.)

of the middle class and to symbolize the liberal faith in the power of education.

The Victorian conviction that scientific genius and technological expertise could create a new earth if not a new heaven is also a recurrent theme of the murals. Yet another worthy cloth merchant, Master William Crabtree, is depicted during the "supreme moment" of observing the transit of Venus over the sun in 1639. Whereas Crabtree's role was only to assist his friend Horrox, the achievement of John Dalton was certainly a great moment in the history of science. This Manchester schoolmaster, who "alone and unassisted made himself the father of modern chemistry" through his invention of atomic theory, is depicted collecting marsh gas (because the investigation of gases was the focus for his attempt to explain why matter combines in some proportions and not in others).[68] The early

DALTON COLLECTING MARSH FIRE GAS · Nº 1

"Dalton Collecting Marsh Fire Gas." (By permission of the Manchester Public Library.)

phases of the industrial revolution that transformed England are re-created in two eighteenth-century scenes. "The Opening of the Bridgewater Canal" depicts the heroic conquest of nature through technology and the consequent benefits for commerce. But "John Kay: Inventor of the Fly Shuttle" suggests that machinery was threatening as well as promising. In the painting, local weavers, infuriated by the new machine that displaced their position and disrupted their culture, are about to storm the house of its inventor. Tradition held that Kay escaped — and this was surely an appropriate irony — only because his wife had him carried out in a wool blanket. Although Brown's exposition of the work states that "but for Kay's simple yet epoch-fixing invention of the shuttle...all the wonders and achievements of steam-weaving would never have been perfected," the image itself dramatizes the potentially disastrous impact of technological advancement.[69]

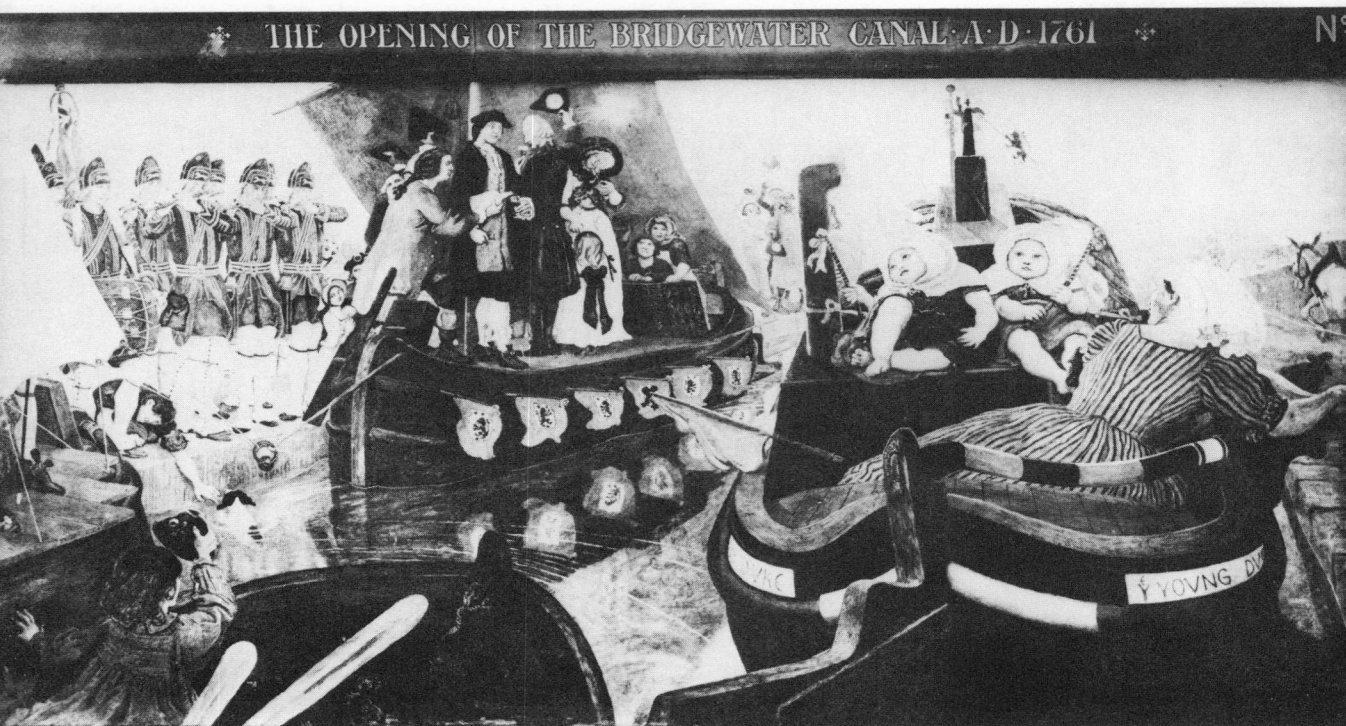

"The Opening of the Bridgewater Canal." (By permission of the Manchester Public Library.)

The tensions between the visual and verbal meanings of "John Kay: Inventor of the Fly Shuttle" brings us to an intriguing issue. The murals do depict the origins of liberal industrial society, charting the progress of Manchester from Agricola to Dalton, but they do not confront the realities of the work-a-day world of the nineteenth century. A controversy that took place in 1878 illuminates the reasons for this striking omission. In March of that year, Ford Madox Brown wrote to Joseph Thompson to tell him that the idea of portraying a contemporary election was, "if not an altogether unpaintable subject...one that would ill supply the place of so stirring an incident as the Peterloo meeting."[70]

Stirring Peterloo certainly was. But several members of the town council did not want to stir up the old animosities produced by the 1819 massacre of workers. It may have seemed wise to screen out the traumatic conflicts of capital and labor

172

JOHN KAY · INVENTOR OF THE FLY SHUTTLE · A·D· 1753   Nº 10

"John Kay: Inventor of the Fly Shuttle." (By permission of the Manchester Public Library.)

that undercut the achievements of industrialism, particularly in a building that was to appeal to men of every rank to help forward the common interest of all. Given the opposition to the Peterloo subject, Joseph Thompson proposed painting the opening of the Bridgewater Canal. This eminently uncontroversial subject proved a good choice, particularly because in the 1880s the municipal leaders of Manchester were involved in a campaign for building a new ship canal to Liverpool.

The story of the Manchester Town Hall needs to be interpreted, finally, in light of John Ruskin's view of "middle-class" Gothic architecture. In 1864 he went to Bradford, at the request of local merchants and manufacturers who wanted his advice on the style of their projected wool exchange. He argued that Bradford – he might as well have said Manchester –

was incapable of creating good architecture because its people worshipped the "goddess of getting on" and had no real desire for beauty. Architecture required adornment by painting or sculpture and these required heroic subjects. "The fact or deed of exchange" was hardly heroic, however, because one man's "getting on" almost inevitably meant the failure of another thousand men. Thus Ruskin sarcastically described the only exchange that was suitable to Bradford, given its values.

> But I can only at present suggest decorating its frieze with pendant purses: and making its pillars broad at the base, for the sticking of bills. And in the innermost chambers of it there might be a Statue of Britannia of the Market...for her spear, she might have a weaver's beam; and on her shield, instead of St. George's Cross, the Milanese boar...and the legend, "In the best market," and her corslet, of leather, folded over her heart in the shape of a purse, with thirty slits in it, for a piece of money to go in at, on each day of the month...And I doubt not but that people would come to see your exchange, and its goddess, with applause.[71]

Both the Manchester Town Hall and the Bradford Wool Exchange represent responses, conscious or unconscious, to Ruskin's position. Their architects and patrons accepted the proposition that architecture requires adornment by painting and sculpture, but the subjects they chose celebrate the romance of industry and the heroism of exchange, neither of which were acceptable to Ruskin.

If the Manchester Town Hall undermined John Ruskin's philosophy of Gothic, it confirmed Walter Bagehot's theory of deference. In *The English Constitution* (1867), Bagehot argued that England was the archetype of the deferential country in which the mass of people yielded obedience to a select few. "Courts and aristocracies," he observed, "have the great quality which rules the multitude, though philosophers can see nothing in it – visibility."[72] Not the aristocratic rulers themselves but the "theatrical show of society" captivated the English people. Patrick Joyce argued that the habit of deference

persisted in the small manufacturing towns of Lancashire both inside and outside the factory.[73] The Manchester Town Hall suggests that his conclusions may also apply in part to the great industrial cities. The middle-class elite of Manchester could not rival the social spectacle of the aristocratic world; but the visual grandeur of their municipal palace was as impressive in its fashion as many a great country house, and as capable of bowing down the imagination. By clothing liberal values in historic dress, the decorations of the Town Hall preempted the reverence granted ordinarily only to the most ancient, venerable institutions. The story of the rise and progress of "Cottonopolis" celebrated ideals and achievements that appealed to different classes. Thus, it defined a local tradition that emphasized the importance of community, not class; whether the common interest was actually middle-class interest in disguise is another question. Yet the Town Hall can be read as an attempt to employ the "dignified" aspects of Manchester's history to impress laboring people with middle-class values and thus maintain middle-class hegemony. There was no better place for the local elite to "educate their masters" than in a citadel of power designed in their own image.

Epilogue:
Traditionalism and industrialism

The face of the past Victorians perceived is significant, finally, for what it reveals about their culture and society. Its meaning needs to be elucidated in the context of changing perspectives on modern British history.

In the nineteenth century, England was seen as the most "bourgeois of nations," both by those like Macaulay, who applauded the middle class, and those like Marx, who affirmed its victory only as a step on the road to socialism. In the Whig interpretation of history, the middle class gained political power through the Reform Bill of 1832 and economic power through industrialism. The triumph of the middle class manifested itself, moreover, in the realm of national values. Evangelicalism, respectability, and self-help shaped the conduct of Victorians as science, technology, and free trade transformed their society. England became the fabled "workshop of the world," renowned for business acumen, inventive genius, political stability, and military might. This vision of Victorian history was challenged by revisionist historians led by George Kitson Clark, who argued that the aristocracy and gentry remained the true masters of English society despite the middle-class challenge.[1] W. D. Rubinstein recently reinforced this conclusion, arguing that the wealthiest men in nineteenth-century England were not northern manufacturers but landowners, followed by financiers, and merchants, who usually had close ties to aristocratic society.[2]

The social problems of Britain in the 1970s and 1980s have spurred a reassessment of the national past. Declining inter-

national prestige and industrial productivity combined with growing political polarization and economic instability have structured perceptions of history. Whereas Whig historiography described the progress of England, outlining the causes of its preeminence and praising those enlightened men responsible for it, now it is more fashionable to analyze the origins of the "British disease," to isolate villains rather than laud heroes.[3] Revisionist historians hold that Britain never became a complete industrial society despite being the first nation to industrialize. The leading proponent of this perspective is Martin J. Wiener, who argued that the "cultural revolution of industrialism," symbolized by the Great Exhibition of 1851, was contained within the traditional culture of landed society. Modern British history, in his view, is essentially the story of the gentrification of the middle class and their acceptance of an upper-class style of life and ethos. Because the aristocracy was flexible enough to grant the new rich a measure of political power and then a degree of social acceptance, they were able to co-opt them. The education provided by the public schools and the ancient universities made the sons of businessmen more at home in the Classics than in the factory. It opened up the prospect of suitably upper-class careers in the civil service, banking, finance, and diplomacy. Wiener traces the long-term decline of Britain from the end of the nineteenth century, when middle- and upper-class elites consolidated into the national elite, later called the Establishment, under the banner of gentry values. Industrialists and financiers tended to sacrifice energetic entrepreneurship for the pursuit of civilized leisure and the struggle for profits for the exercise of good form. The culture of the first industrial society was, ironically, more concerned with the country than the city, more with the past than the future.[4]

This powerful case requires careful qualification. It is certainly correct in stressing the persistence of aspects of a status society based on hierarchy, deference, and land; and in stressing the ambivalent responses to industrialism in nineteenth- and twentieth-century England. The problem is that it over-

looks certain complexities of the "English way of life" by assuming that cultural characteristics such as the appreciation of history and the idealization of nature were intrinsically antimodern forces. Yet I argue in this book that this is only one side of the picture: Liberal England's middle-class politicians and businessmen appropriated medieval forms to create pedigrees for their values and to legitimize their quest for hegemony. Although their concern with historic paraphernalia superficially reinforced the authority of traditional symbols, actually it diminished the prescriptive force of the past by reinterpreting its meanings in light of progressive aspirations. The gentrification of the middle class is an ambiguous process: It reveals as much about the mystification of industrial capitalism as about its domestication. What is perhaps most telling about the cultural activities analyzed in this book is that none of them posed a fundamental threat to the business world.

Whether English cultural values contributed to the decline of England's economic power is still very much an open question. The following examples suggest, however, that the concern with the past did not conflict directly with the progress of modernization. What César Graña said of museums applies equally well to Victorian archeology and tourism: If they aroused emotions of homage, they did not lead to subservience to the ancestral.[5] There is no reason to assume that a Bradford businessman would have been any less dedicated an entrepreneur, or any less interested in profits, for having an interest in collecting Roman coins. Along with his fellow traders he carried out his business in Bradford's Neo-Gothic Wool Exchange, surrounded by images of the legends of Bishop Blaize and the early history of the wool trade. But if the setting was "medieval," the business methods and goals were decidedly modern. The rehabilitation of Gothic architecture in Manchester served rather than impeded the requirements of an "advanced civilization" by housing a burgeoning bureaucracy and glorifying the values of provincial liberalism. The Manchester Town Hall assimilated the taste for Gothic architecture propagated by John Ruskin and William Morris by dissociating the

179

style from the philosophy on which it was founded. Gothic forms beautified industrial Manchester without changing its social structure. The preservation of ancient buildings was, in one sense, symptomatic of nostalgia for the past and dissatisfaction with the industrial landscape. Yet it also exemplified the idea that "men restore what they cease to resent."[6] Preserving the architectural survivals of the Middle Ages did not require commitment to its institutions or ideals; indeed, by the 1870s Victorians could safely preserve remnants of the medieval past because "feudalism" posed little threat to their civilization. It is true that there were sometimes conflicts between saving the past and building the future, as the story of the city churches of York proves. These conflicts were minimized, however, by selecting specific monuments for preservation and forsaking the rest.

Rural fantasies were also incorporated into an urban society. Although Ruskin accused his contemporaries of "destroying Nature," he also recognized how they compensated for the loss. "We find all men of true feeling," he observed, "delighting to escape out of modern cities into natural scenery."[7] The Victorian city dwellers' love of nature manifested itself in their parks and zoos, their seaside holidays, their garden suburbs, and their rustic cottages. Those who could not afford rural retreats or suburban villas found other ways to bring the country to the city. Take, for instance, Mrs. Plornish in Dickens's *Little Dorrit* (1857), the wife of a workman, who lived in a section of London called Bleeding Heart Yard. Unable to move to the thatch-roof country cottage she dreamed of, she instead hired a scene painter to create a mural that depicted her ideal. The mural portrayed the exterior of a cottage graced with hollyhocks and sunflowers. In addition,

> a quantity of dense smoke issuing from the chimney indicated good cheer within . . . A faithful dog was represented . . . and a circular pigeon-house, enveloped in a cloud of pigeons, arose from behind the garden-paling. On the door appeared the semblance of a brass

plate, presenting the inscription, Happy Cottage, T. and M. Plornish.[8]

This archetypal image of a happy family living close to nature would be an ideal expression of Victorians' dreams were the cottage in question a picturesque variety of Gothic architecture.

It is customary for foreign and inland observers alike to emphasize the importance of tradition in British society. Walter Bagehot recognized the tendency of the English to accord respect to what was known to be old rather than what had proved to be good.[9] Yet this did not prevent him from seeing that venerable traditions were neither unchanging nor seamless. For Bagehot, the English Constitution was "ancient and ever-altering"; he likened it to an "old man who still wears with attached fondness clothes in the fashion of his youth: what you see of him is the same; what you do not see is wholly altered."[10] And that is precisely the point: Victorians recast and reinterpreted traditional symbols and values, often by preserving their forms while altering their functions. Tradition and modernity have often been antithetical terms in sociological theory, but their relationship in historical reality has been more complex.[11] The conflicts between the traditional and modern elements of English life were mitigated by infusing new meanings into historic forms, by incorporating aspects of the preindustrial world into a new cultural framework, and by relegating potentially antimodern forces to the realms of art, leisure, and ritual. Traditional practices had considerable sway in the ceremonial sphere of political life but negligible impact in the practical world of technology. The celebration of nature and history assumed forms that did not interfere directly with the work-a-day world: Restful weekends spent in the countryside touring old churches may well have helped the English adapt to aspects of contemporary society that they found unappealing and uninspiring. This is not to say that the life of the countryside and the life of the city, the past and the present were never at odds. Yet Victorians

brought them together in garden suburbs lined with Gothic, Tudor, and Queen Anne villas and surrounded with luxuriant greenery; and in museums filled with the relics of the past and the spoils of imperialism. In building a new civilization, Victorians altered the face of the past to suit the needs of modern life; their inheritance proved eminently portable and its history is not yet complete.

Abbreviations used in notes

AL-MCRL	Autograph Letters Collections, Manchester Central Reference Library, Manchester
BHAS	Bradford Historical and Antiquarian Society, Bradford Central Reference Library, Bradford
LLHL	Leeds Local History Library, Leeds Central Reference Library, Leeds
MLHL	Manchester Local History Library, Manchester Central Library, Manchester
KA-SPAB	Kirkstall Abbey File, Society for the Protection of Ancient Buildings, London
SAS	Sussex Archaeological Society, Lewes
SPAB	Society for the Protection of Ancient Buildings, London
SPAB Report	Annual Report of the Society for the Protection of Ancient Buildings, London
YAS	Yorkshire Archaeological Society, Leeds
YCC-SPAB	York City Churches File, Society for the Protection of Ancient Buildings, London

Notes

1. THE PARADOXES OF PROGRESS

1 Carroll Meeks, *The Railroad Station: An Architectural History* (New Haven: Yale University Press, 1956).

2 It is, of course, debatable when the Middle Ages began and ended. The justification for the definition of the Middle Ages as a period stretching from the fifth to the fifteenth centuries comes from contemporary usage, notably that of John Ruskin. See *Oxford English Dictionary*, 3rd ed., s.v. "mediaevalism." As for other terms, "Liberal" refers to a partisan of the Liberal Party; "liberal" refers to a broader set of values favorable to science, technology, industrialism, and free trade.

3 See Arthur O. Lovejoy, "The First Gothic Revival and the Return to Nature," *Modern Language Notes* XLVII (May 1932):419–46.

4 On the Romantics see especially Hugh Honour, *Romanticism* (New York: Harper & Row, 1979), pp. 156–216; W. D. Robson-Scott, *The Literary Background of the Gothic Revival in Germany* (Oxford: Oxford University Press, 1965); Kenneth Clark, *The Gothic Revival: An Essay in the History of Taste* (New York: Harper & Row, 1962); and Gottfried Saloman, *Das Mittelalter als Ideal in der Romantik* (Munich: Drei Masken Verlag, 1922).

5 *Oxford English Dictionary*, 3rd ed. s.v. "mediaeval," "mediaevally," "mediaevalist," and "mediaevalize."

6 *The Illustrated London News*, 21 September 1845, 8 November 1845.

7 Frederic Harrison, *Autobiographical Memoirs*, 2 vols. (London: Macmillan, 1911), I:225–6.

8 For the reconstruction of the City see John Summerson, "London the Artifact," in *The Victorian City: Images and Reality*, ed. H. J. Dyos and Michael Wolff, 2 vols. (London: Routledge & Kegan Paul, 1978), II:315.

9 See the excellent analyses of these writers in Raymond Williams, *Culture and Society, 1780–1950* (New York: Harper & Row, 1966), pp. 139–62.

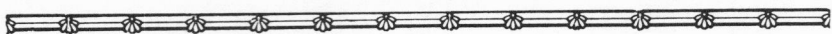

10 See the classic essay by Christopher Hill, "The Norman Yoke," in *Democracy and the Labour Movement*, ed. John Saville (London: Laurence & Wisehart, 1954), pp. 66–110.

11 See W.R.W. Stephens, *The Life and Letters of Edward Freeman*, 2 vols. (London, 1895), II:21, 43.

12 Ibid., pp. 200–1.

13 His political interests and opinions are a major theme of his correspondence. For examples see Edward Freeman to James Bryce, 29 April 1866, 3 February 1867, in Bryce Papers 4:95, 120, Bodleian University Library, Oxford University, Oxford, England; and Edward Freeman to William Gladstone, 24 December 1865, Gladstone Papers, Add. MSS. 44408, p. 264, the British Library, London, England.

14 Edward Freeman to James Bryce, 8 September 1867, Bryce Papers 4:166.

15 Edward Freeman, *The Growth of the English Constitution from the Earliest Times*, 3rd ed. (London, 1876), p. iii.

16 Ibid., p. x.

17 Ibid., p. 59.

18 For example, see Mark Girouard, *Life in the English Country House: A Social and Architectural History* (New Haven: Yale University Press, 1978).

19 E. P. Thompson, *William Morris: Romantic to Revolutionary* (London: Merlin Press, 1977), pp. 9, 27–39.

20 Asa Briggs, *Victorian People: A Reassessment of Persons and Themes, 1851–67* (Harmondsworth, Middlesex: Penguin Books, 1965), p. 47.

21 Clifford Geertz, *The Interpretation of Culture* (New York: Basic Books, 1973), pp. 21–2.

22 On the functions of historical consciousness see especially J. H. Plumb, *The Death of the Past* (Boston: Houghton Mifflin, 1970); and Bernard Lewis, *History: Remembered, Recovered, Invented* (Princeton: Princeton University Press, 1976).

23 The concept of tradition used here was heavily influenced by Raymond Williams, *Marxism and Literature* (Oxford: Oxford University Press, 1978), pp. 108–128.

24 The discussion of the functions of tradition is deeply indebted to S. N. Eisenstadt, *Tradition, Change and Modernity* (New York: Wiley, 1973), chap. 1.

25 See Eric Hobsbawm's extremely suggestive article "The Social Function of the Past: Some Questions," *Past and Present* 55 (May 1972):2–17; Philip Abrams, "The Sense of the Past and the Origins of Sociology," *Past and Present* 55 (May 1972):18–22; and Francis Haskell, "The Manufacture of the Past in 19th Century Painting," *Past and Present* 53 (November 1971):109–120.

26 See Eisenstadt, *Tradition, Change and Modernity*, p. 351.

27 Karl Marx and Friedrich Engels, *Basic Writings on Politics and Philosophy*, ed. Lewis S. Feuer (Garden City, N.Y.: Doubleday/Anchor Books, 1949), p. 320.

28 Ibid., p. 322.

29 Lord Acton quoted in Herbert Butterfield, *Man on His Past: The Study of the History of Historical Scholarship* (Cambridge: Cambridge University Press, 1969), p. 212. On classicism see Richard Jenkyns, *The Victorians and Ancient Greece* (Oxford: Blackwell, 1980).

30 See Asa Briggs, *Victorian People*, pp. 19–20; and Martin J. Wiener, *English Culture and the Decline of the Industrial Spirit, 1850–1980* (Cambridge: Cambridge University Press, 1981), pp. 3–25.

31 Walter Bagehot, *The English Constitution*, Introduction by R.H.S. Crossman (Ithaca: Cornell University Press, 1966), p. 122.

32 W. D. Rubinstein, "Wealth, Elites and the Class Structure of Modern Britain," *Past and Present* 76 (August 1977):99–126, and "The Victorian Middle Classes: Wealth, Occupation and Geography," *Economic History Review*, ser. 2, 30 (1977):602–32.

33 Thomas Hardy, *Tess of the D'Urbervilles* (1891; New York: Norton, 1979), p. 32.

2. THE VISION OF HISTORY

1 The documentary sources are drawn from the General Correspondence and the Hoper Letters, SAS.

2 General Correspondence, 46/29–35, SAS.

3 M. A. Lower, "Report on the Antiquities Lately Found at Lewes," *Journal of the British Archaeological Association* I (1846), p. 352.

4 *The Illustrated London News*, 8 November 1845.

5 Ibid.

6 Ibid.

7 Wellseley to Blaauw, 19 November 1845; Gaunt to Hoper, undated, General Correspondence, 45/4, 10, SAS.

8 Blaauw to Hoper, 6 December 1845, Hoper Letters, H/17, SAS.

9 Correspondents unknown, 12 February 1846, General Correspondence, 46/6, SAS.

10 Lower to Blaauw, undated 1849, General Correspondence, 49/4, SAS. See also Mark Antony Lower, *A Handbook for Lewes, Historical and Descriptive* (London, 1845).

11 William Figg, "On the Relics Found at Lewes," *Sussex Archaeological Collections* I (1848):45; Blaauw to Lower, undated, General Correspondence, 46/21, SAS.

12 On the sense of place see Asa Briggs, "The Sense of Place," in *The Fitness of Man's Environment*, Smithsonian Annual, vol. II (Washington: Smithsonian Institute, 1968), pp. 77–99; and Kevin Lynch, *The Image of the City* (Cambridge, Mass.: MIT Press, 1960).

13 Report reprinted from *Wakefield Express*, 25 August 1869, as "Excursion to Wakefield," Yorkshire Archaeological and Topographical Society Excursions I:17, YAS.

14 Yorkshire Archaeological and Topographical Society Excursions I:6, YAS.

15 On eighteenth-century attitudes and activities see Esther Moir, *The Discovery of Britain: The English Tourists* (London: Routledge & Kegan Paul, 1964).

16 *Oxford English Dictionary*, 3rd ed., s.v. "sightsee," "tour," "tourist."

17 *The Handbook for Hastings, St. Leonard's and Their Neighbourhood* (Hastings, 1845), p. iii.

18 *The Historical Guide to Leeds* (Leeds, 1858), p. 2.

19 *British Association for the Advancement of Science Guide to Sheffield* (Sheffield, 1879).

20 They were reprinted as John Doran, *Memoirs of Our Great Towns* (London, 1878).

21 See Yorkshire Archaeological and Topographical Society Excursions I, YAS.

22 "Excursion to Wakefield," Yorkshire Archaeological and Topographical Society Excursions I:8–17, YAS.

23 "Excursion to Wakefield," Yorkshire Archaeological and Topographical Society Excursions I:18, YAS.

24 "Excursion to Mount Grace Priory," Yorkshire Archaeological and Topographical Society Excursions I:n.p., YAS.

25 "Excursion to Wakefield," Yorkshire Archaeological and Topographical Society Excursions I:5, YAS.

26 Quoted in G. P. Gooch, *History and Historians in the Nineteenth Century* (Boston: Beacon Press, 1959), p. 265.

27 For the Rolls Series see ibid., pp. 265–71.

28 For pre-Victorian developments see Stuart Piggott, *William Stukeley* (Oxford: Oxford University Press/Clarendon Press, 1950); idem, *Ruins in a Landscape* (Edinburgh: University of Edinburgh Press, 1976); Joan Evans, *History of the Society of Antiquaries* (Oxford: Oxford University Press, 1956); Esther Moir, *The Discovery of Britain: The English Tourists* (London: Routledge & Kegan Paul, 1964); and T. D. Kendrick, *British Antiquity* (London: Methuen, 1950).

29 Cf. Stuart Piggott, "The Origins of the English County Archaeological Societies," in *Ruins in a Landscape*, pp. 171–95. This article is useful on the relationship between the Anglican Revival and antiquarianism as well as on the relationship between geology and archeology. The author emphasizes the vogue of antiquarianism in conservative Anglican regions.

30 On the class structure of Manchester see especially Derek Fraser, *Urban Politics in Victorian England: The Structure of Politics in Victorian Cities* (Leicester: Leicester University Press, 1976).

31 The major sources of the histories of these societies include the Transactions of the Bradford Historical and Antiquarian Society, BHAS; Yorkshire Archaeological and Topographical Society Minute Books, YAS; and Sussex Archaeological Society Transactions, SAS.

32 General Correspondence, 46/43, SAS; and *Sussex Express*, 30 May 1846.

33 W. H. Blaauw, "On Sussex Archaeology," *Sussex Archaeological Collections* I (1848):1.

34 For the social composition of these two groups see Membership Lists, YAS, and Membership Lists, SAS.

35 Membership Lists, BHAS.

36 See the report in the *Sussex Advertiser*, 26 May 1846.

37 Blaauw, "On Sussex Archaeology."

38 Ibid., p. 2.

39 See the report in the *Huddersfield Chronicle*, 10 June 1865.

40 Ibid.

41 Sussex Archaeological Society Transactions I:47, SAS.

42 James Wardell, *An Historical Account of Kirkstall Abbey* (Leeds, 1865), p. 12.

43 *Huddersfield Chronicle*, 10 June 1865.

44 See the report in the *Sussex Advertiser*, 26 May 1846.

45 Report in *Leeds Intelligencer*, 31 August 1882.

46 See *The Bradford Antiquary* (1888–), *Yorkshire Archaeological and Topographical Journal* (1870–), and *Sussex Archaeological Collections* (1848–).

47 For examples see "On the Seals of the Sussex Cinque Ports," *Sussex Archaeological Collections* II (1849):15–16; "Roman Remains Discovered at New Haven in 1852," *Sussex Archaeological Collections* V (1852):252–6; "On the Roman Station at Slack," *Yorkshire Archaeological and Topographical Journal* I (1870):1–10; "Inscriptions on Church Bells of the East Riding of Yorkshire," *Yorkshire Archaeological and Topographical Journal* II (1873): 82–6; "Copies of Inscriptions in the Bradford Parish Church," *The Bradford Antiquary* I (1888):51–233.

48 For instances see "On the Characteristic Features of Chichester Cathedral," *Sussex Archaeological Collections* I (1848):38–53; "Memorials of the Town, Parish and Cinque-Port of Seaford," *Sussex Archaeological Collections* VII (1854):73–152; "Ancient Pedigree of the Hanson Family," *Yorkshire Archaeological Journal* II (1873); "On the Painted Glass at Thornhill," *Yorkshire Archaeological and Topographical Journal* I (1870):69–78; "Eminent Townsmen of Pudsey," *The Bradford Antiquary* I (1888):33–8.

49 See "Almondsbury in Feudal Times," *Yorkshire Archaeological and Topographical Journal* II (1873):1–34; "Biographical Notes on Yorkshire Tenants Named in Domesday Book," *Yorkshire Archaeological and Topographical Journal* IV (1877):215–40; "On the Battle of Hastings," *Sussex Archaeological Collections* IV (1854):15–40; "On the Nonae of 1340, as Relating to Sussex," *Sussex Archaeological Collections* I (1848):58–64; "Bradford in the Middle of the Fourteenth Century," *The Bradford Antiquary* I (1888):4–9.

50 See Neil Smelser, *Social Change in the Industrial Revolution: An Application of Theory to the Lancashire Cotton Industry 1770–1840* (Chicago: University of Chicago Press, 1959).

51 The compliment was paid by a local newspaper, *Sussex Express*, 30 May 1846.

52 On the birth of class see Asa Briggs, "The Language of Class in Early 19th Century England," in *Essays in Labour History*, ed. Asa Briggs and John Saville (London: Macmillan, 1960), pp. 43–73; and Harold Perkin, *The Origins of Modern English Society 1780–1880* (Toronto: University of Toronto Press, 1972), pp. 176–218.

53 On provincialism as a cultural, social, and political force see Asa Briggs, *Victorian Cities* (Harmondsworth, Middlesex: Penguin Books, 1975). Also useful is Donald Read, *The English Provinces* (London: Arnold, 1964).

54 *Huddersfield Chronicle*, 10 June 1865.

55 Yorkshire Archaeological and Topographical Society Minute Book I:34, YAS.

56 Mark Antony Lower, *Chronicles of Pevensey* (Lewes, London, 1846), p. ii.

57 Mandell Creighton, *Carlisle* (London, 1889), p. vi.

58 G. W. Kitchin, *Winchester* (London, 1890), pp. vii, 222.

59 Creighton, *Carlisle*, p. 203.

60 Montagu Burrows, *Cinque Ports* (London, 1895), p. 2.

61 *The Exeter Guide and Itinerary* (Exeter, 1836), n.p.

62 William Hunt, *Bristol* (London, 1889), p. 222.

63 *Tourist's Picturesque Guide to Nottingham and Its Environs* (Nottingham, 1871), p. 8.

64 Kitchin, *Winchester*, p. iv.

65 E. L. Cutts, *Colchester* (London, 1888), p. 1.

66 *Handbook for Hastings and St. Leonard's*, p. 14.

67 *Exeter Guide and Itinerary*, p. 7.

68 Guidebooks covered entire counties as well as particular towns. See, for example, *Ready Guide and Tourist's Handbook for Sussex* (London, 1878), p. 7.

69 *Exeter Guide and Itinerary*, p. 7.

70 Kitchin, *Winchester*, p. 159.

71 Hunt, *Bristol*, p. 3.

72 On the nationalization of provincial cultures see Briggs, *Victorian Cities*, p. 43.

73 *The Handy Guide to Bradford* (Bradford, 1873), p. iv.

74 On the relationship between the upper-middle class and the aristocracy see S. G. Checkland, *The Rise of Industrial Society in England, 1815–1885* (London: Longman, 1971), pp. 284–5.

75 J. W. Turner, "Some Old Bradford Firms," *The Bradford Antiquary* I (1888):138.

76 *Old Leeds: Its Bygones and Celebrities, By an Old Leeds Cropper* (Leeds, 1868), p. 18. The Leeds Radical was, most probably, Jeremiah Odham.

77 *Historical Guide to Leeds*, p. 9.

78 See especially *Handy Guide to Bradford* and *Handbook to Bradford and the Neighbourhood* (Bradford, 1873).

79 *Guide to Manchester and Salford* (Edinburgh, 1879), p. 4. See also *A*

Description of Manchester (Manchester, 1860); James Tait, *Medieval Manchester and the Beginnings of Lancashire* (Manchester, 1849); *Manchester As It Is* (Manchester, 1839); *The Manchester Guide* (Manchester, 1804).

80 R. L. Kirby, *Ancient Middlesbrough: Gleanings of Local History* (Middlesbrough, 1900), p. 12.

81 *Handbook to Bradford*, p. 14.

82 Ibid., p. 189.

83 See John James, *History of the Worsted Manufacture in England* (Bradford, 1857); and Edward Collinson, *The History of the Worsted Trade and the Historic Sketch of Bradford* (London, 1854).

84 James, *Worsted Manufacture in England*, pp. 62–3.

85 Matthew Arnold, *Culture and Anarchy* (London, 1869), chap. 1.

86 Quoted in Briggs, *Victorian Cities*, p. 379. See Briggs's criticism of Mumford's views.

87 "Excursion to York," Yorkshire Archaeological and Topographical Journal I:5, YAS.

88 Freeman wrote extensively on both local and national history, as in his *English Towns and Districts* (London, 1883) and his *Growth of the English Constitution from the Earliest Times*, 3rd ed. (1870; London 1876).

89 Elizabeth Markham, *History of England* (London, 1863), p. 1.

90 Mandell Creighton, *The English National Character* (Oxford, 1896), p. 15.

91 Cyril Ransome, *Elementary History of England* (London, 1890), p. vi.

92 Asa Briggs, *Saxons, Normans and Victorians* (Hastings: Historical Association, 1966), p. 3.

93 For Harrison's view of Alfred see Frederic Harrison, *The Writings of King Alfred* (London: Macmillan, 1901), and *The Millenary of King Alfred* (Birmingham, 1897).

94 The major source on the planning and execution of the millenary is Alfred Bowker, *The Millenary of King Alfred* (London: Macmillan, 1902).

95 Ibid., pp. 9, 11.

96 Ibid., p. 23.

97 Briggs, *Victorian Cities*, p. 43.

98 Bowker, *Millenary of King Alfred*, p. iii.

99 Ibid., pp. 3, 9, 13, 31.

100 Ibid., pp. 109–10.

101 Ibid., pp. 147–8.

102 Ibid., p. 107.

103 Ibid., p. 101.

104 Ibid., photographic facsimile, facing p. 190.

105 Ibid., photographic facsimile, facing p. 28.

106 Ibid., p. 188.

107 Ibid., p. 187.

108 Ibid., p. 188.

3. THE PRESERVATION OF THE PAST

1 For his speech see SPAB Report (1887), pp. 65–77.

2 Frederic Harrison, *Autobiographical Memoirs*, 2 vols. (London: Macmillan, 1911), I:51–3.

3 His essays on London and Paris are conveniently reprinted in Frederic Harrison, *The Meaning of History* (London, 1894), pp. 368–436.

4 For the correspondence see Peterborough Town Hall File, SPAB.

5 For their reactions and those of many others see the Records of the St. Mark's Committee, Add. MSS. 38831, the British Library, London, and St. Mark's, Venice File, SPAB.

6 *Daily News*, 3 November 1879.

7 On late-nineteenth-century Birmingham and its civic gospel see Conrad Gill and Asa Briggs, *The History of Birmingham*, vol. II (Oxford: Oxford University Press, 1952).

8 The meeting is thoroughly reported in *Birmingham Daily Post*, 14 November 1879.

9 For discussions of Victorian restorations see Jane Fawcett, "A Restoration Tragedy: Cathedrals in the Eighteenth and Nineteenth Centuries," and Mark Girouard, "Living with the Past: Victorian Alterations to Country Houses," in *The Future of the Past*, ed. Jane Fawcett (London: Thames & Hudson, 1976), pp. 75–116, 117–40.

10 For the Ecclesiologists see James F. White, *The Cambridge Movement: The Ecclesiologists and the Gothic Revival* (Cambridge: Cambridge University Press, 1962), pp. 25–47.

11 Quoted in ibid., p. 159.

12 Ibid., pp. 161–2.

13 Peter Ferriday, "The Church Restorers," *Architectural Review* CXXXVI (1964):87.

14 *Building News* IV (1858).

15 Mark Girouard, "Living with the Past," p. 135.

16 For Ruskin's and Scott's attitudes see Nikolaus Pevsner, "Scrape and Anti-Scrape," in *The Future of the Past*, ed. Fawcett, pp. 44–50.

17 SPAB Report (1882), p. 23.

18 For the shift in taste and its relationship to historic preservation see Mark Girouard, "Living with the Past," p. 135. See also Mark Girouard, *Sweetness and Light: The 'Queen Anne' Movement 1860–1900* (Oxford: Oxford University Press, 1977), pp. 1–38.

19 SPAB Report (1877), p. 9.

20 Ibid., p. 20.

21 *Athaenaeum*, 5 March 1877.

22 Ibid.

23 *Fun*, 27 July 1877.

24 *Punch*, 8 September 1877.

25 SPAB Report (1878), p. 6.

26 Ibid. (1885), pp. 65–6.

27 Ibid. (1882), p. 35, and ibid. (1885), pp. 51–4.

28 Ibid. (1882), p. 26.

29 Ibid. (1904), p. 76.

30 Ibid. (1878), p. 20.

31 Ibid. (1878), p. 71.

32 Ibid. (1878), p. 7.

33 Ibid. (1887), p. 57.

34 Ibid. (1887), p. 79.

35 Philip H. Delamotte and Joseph Cundall, *A Photographic Tour among the Abbeys of Yorkshire* (London, 1856), p. 11.

36 For the architectural and historical background see W. H. St. John Hope and John Bilson, "Architectural Description of Kirkstall Abbey," *The Publications of the Thoresby Society* XVI (1907):1–140.

37 Kevin Lynch produced intriguing results by interviewing the residents of contemporary American cities. See his study, *The Image of the City* (Cambridge, Mass.: MIT Press, 1960), chap. II.

38 See "An Elegy upon the Ruins of Kirkstall Abbey," Kirkstall Abbey Collection, LLHL.

39 "Kirkstall Abbey," Kirkstall Abbey Collection, LLHL.

40 Dr. John Ryley Robinson, "Kirkstall Abbey," Kirkstall Abbey Collection, LLHL.

41 Quoted in Delamotte and Cundall, *Abbeys of Yorkshire*, p. 15.

42 "A Lecture for the People," Kirkstall Abbey Collection, LLHL.

43 G. G. Scott, *Kirkstall Abbey and Its Restoration* (London, 1873). It is also notable that Akroyd was the founder of Akroydon, a model factory community on the Yorkshire moors that used Neo-Gothic architecture to strengthen "house and home attachment." On this point see Edward Akroyd, *On Improved Dwellings for the Working Classes* (London, 1862), p. 8.

44 "A Lecture for the People."

45 For a useful survey of the debates on the various parliamentary bills see Wayland Young, *Preservations* (London: Smith, 1972), chap. 1.

46 See Ellen Heaton to Thackeray Turner, 18 September 1882, and Edmund Berchall to Thackeray Turner, 8 September 1882, KA-SPAB.

47 W. C. Marshall to Thackeray Turner, 21 June 1883, KA-SPAB.

48 Thackeray Turner to B. E. Bennett, 10 October 1882, KA-SPAB.

49 On Wilson see E. P. Hennock, *Fit and Proper Persons: Ideal and Reality in Nineteenth Century Urban Government* (London: Arnold, 1973), pp. 234, 236, 242, 244–5.

50 W. C. Marshall to Thackeray Turner, 21 June 1883, KA-SPAB.

51 See Turner's Letter to the Editor, *Leeds Mercury*, 12 September 1888.

52 Undated clipping, SPAB.

53 *Birmingham Daily Post*, 20 August 1888.

54 *Leeds Mercury*, 13 September 1888.

55 Ibid.

56 See letters in *Yorkshire Post*, 25 August 1888.

57 *Leeds Mercury*, 4 September 1888.

58 Ibid., 4 September 1888.

59 *Metropolitan*, 5 December 1888.

60 For the various rumors see *Times* (London), 16 January 1889, and *Yorkshire Evening Post*, 22 December 1888.

61 For North's role see *Times* (London), 16 January 1889.

62 *Leeds Mercury*, 1 September 1888; *Yorkshire Evening Post*, 22 October 1888; *Birmingham Daily Post*, 12 August 1888.

63 *Yorkshire Evening Post*, 14 September 1888.

64 *Birmingham Daily Post*, 20 August 1888.

65 For the quest see Walter L. Creese, "Imagination in the Suburb," in *Nature and the Victorian Imagination*, ed. U. C. Knoepflmacher and G. B. Tennyson (Berkeley: University of California Press, 1977), pp. 49–68.

66 See his Letter to the Editor, *Leeds Mercury*, 4 September 1888.

67 Ibid.

68 Ibid., 12 October 1888.

69 *Yorkshire Evening Post*, 25 August 1888.

70 *Leeds Mercury*, 1 September 1888.

71 *Yorkshire Evening Post*, 22 December 1888.

72 *Newscastle Chronicle*, 17 December 1888.

73 *Metropolitan*, 15 December 1888.

74 The politics involved in the restoration can be glimpsed in W. H. St. John Hope to Thackeray Turner, 7 December 1889, 15 June 1892; Mickelthwaite to Thackeray Turner, 1 June 1892, 11 July 1893; correspondent unknown, 23 October 1894; Thackeray Turner to Town Clerk of Leeds, 21 May 1881; all of which are in KA-SPAB. Also see the interesting editorial in *Leeds Mercury*, 5 February 1890.

75 See Washington Teasdale's Letter to the Editor, *Leeds Mercury*, 6 February 1890.

76 Letter to SPAB, unknown correspondent, 23 October 1894, KA-SPAB.

77 See the detailed report of the opening ceremonies in *Leeds Mercury*, 16 September 1895.

78 See the volume by James Raine, *York* (London, 1890).

79 Although there is no recent scholarly study of the social milieu of late-Victorian York, there is much of value in Alan Armstrong, *Stability and Change in an English Country Town: A Social Study of York 1801–51* (Cambridge: Cambridge University Press, 1974).

80 See *A New Description of York* (York, 1825); *A Guide for Strangers and Residents in York* (York, 1842); *The Visitor's Guide to the Cathedral and City of York* (York, 1869); *Illustrated Penny Guide to York* (York, 1879).

81 See the report in *York Herald*, 29 July 1874.

82 Ibid.

83 For the details of the report see *York Herald*, 2 February 1885, 12 February 1885; *Yorkshire Gazette*, 11 February 1885.

84 The able biography of the archbishop hardly mentions the York city churches affair. See Harold Kirk-Smith, *William Thomson, Archbishop of York, His Life and Times* (London: Society for the Promotion of Christian Knowledge, 1958).

85 On the churches see *Yorkshire Gazette*, 11 February 1885; *The Churches of York* (York, 1843).

86 See the Poster, YCC-SPAB.

87 Newton Mant to Thackeray Turner, 17 February 1885, YCC-SPAB.

88 Newton Mant to Thackeray Turner, 1 June 1885, YCC-SPAB.

89 For Mant's opinion of the man he called a "crafty scoundrel" and the like, see Newton Mant to Thackeray Turner, 17 February 1885, 8 March 1885, YCC-SPAB.

90 For Mant's strategy see Newton Mant to Thackeray Turner, 2 March 1885, 20 April 1885, YCC-SPAB. For his low opinion of the taste of the people of York see Newton Mant to Thackeray Turner, 17 February 1885, YCC-SPAB.

91 George Trundle to SPAB, 4 April 1885, YCC-SPAB.

92 For Raine's position see Newton Mant to Thackeray Turner, 8 March 1886, 6 May 1886; J. T. Mickelthwaite to Thackeray Turner, 27 August 1885, YCC-SPAB.

93 See T. W. Norwood to Thackeray Turner, 4 March 1885; Arthur J. Munby to SPAB, 23 April 1885; S. H. Bennett to Newton Mant, 6 April 1885, YCC-SPAB.

94 See Thackeray Turner's Letter to the Editor, *Yorkshire Post*, 27 February 1888.

95 Wallace Hargrove to George Howard, 11 March 1885, YCC-SPAB.

96 The Archbishop of York to Lord Herries, 19 March 1885, YCC-SPAB.

97 For Hargrove's shift see Wallace Hargrove to George Howard, 11 March 1885; Wallace Hargrove to Newton Mant, 7 August 1885, YCC-SPAB. Also see the report of the public meeting in York concerning the churches in *York Herald*, 1 June 1885.

98 See his letter in *York Herald*, 12 March 1885.

99 Newton Mant to Thackeray Turner, 4 May, 6 May, 22 May 1885, YCC-SPAB.

100 Newton Mant to Thackeray Turner, 13 March 1885, 22 May 1885, YCC-SPAB.

101 See the report of the meeting in *York Herald*, 1 June 1885.

102 See his letter, ibid., 17 March.

103 Ibid., 1 June 1888.

104 Richard Grosvenor to Thackeray Turner, 3 June 1885, YCC-SPAB.

105 *Truth*, 17 September 1885.

106 *Saturday Review*, 19 September 1885; *Manchester Guardian*, 22 September 1885; *Antiquary*, April 1885; *Notes and Queries*, 6 June 1885; *Weekly Churchman and Home Reunion*, 29 February 1885, 20 June 1885.

107 See *Times* (London), 10 September, 16 September 1885. The archbishop

also had acrimonious exchanges with ecclesiastical organizations such as the Free and Open Church Association. See Archbishop of York to Rev. Bowater Vernon, 16 July 1885, YCC-SPAB.

108 Kevin Lynch, *What Time Is This Place?* (Cambridge, Mass.: MIT Press, 1972).

4. THE ARCHITECTURE OF THE INDUSTRIAL CITY

1 Cecil Stewart, *The Stones of Manchester* (London: Arnold, 1956), provides much useful information on the local Gothic Revival.

2 For the Manchester of the 1840s see Asa Briggs, *Victorian Cities* (Harmondsworth, Middlesex: Penguin Books, 1975), pp. 88–138; and Steven Marcus, *Engels, Manchester and the Working Class* (New York: Vintage Books, 1974), pp. 28–66.

3 See Dorothy Shena Simon, *A Century of City Government* (London: Allen & Unwin, 1938), p. 339, for the cathedral comparison. It was conventional to see the New Town Hall as the "architectural and municipal center" of Manchester. See, for instance, *Manchester Courier*, 10 September 1877.

4 See *Builder*, 9 January 1875.

5 "Architects," in E. H. Pitcairn, *The Unwritten Laws and Ideals of Active Careers* (London, 1899), p. 343.

6 For contemporary descriptions of the building see especially William Axon, *An Architectural and General Description of the Town Hall, Manchester* (Manchester, 1878), pp. 1–40; *Manchester Guardian*, 5 September 1877; *Builder*, 9 January 1875. Of special interest is Waterhouse's own description of the building. See the report in *Builder*, 24 February 1877.

7 See the report of the meeting: *Architect*, 8 June 1878.

8 Axon, *Architectural and General Description*, pp. 2–3.

9 *Builder*, 26 August 1905.

10 See his address to the Royal Institute of British Architects as reported in *Building News*, 15 April 1859.

11 It is described in Axon, *Architectural and General Description*, p. 50.

12 Roger Dixon and Stefan Muthesius, *Victorian Architecture* (New York: Oxford University Press, 1978), p. 151.

13 For the aesthetic setting see M. H. Port, ed., *The Houses of Parliament* (New Haven: Yale University Press, 1976); Peter Collins, *Changing Ideals in Modern Architecture, 1750–1950* (London: Faber & Faber, 1965); Stefan Muthesius, *The High Victorian Movement in Architecture, 1850–70* (London: Routledge & Kegan Paul, 1972); John Summerson, *Victorian Architecture: Four Studies in Evaluation* (New York: Columbia University Press, 1971).

14 General Proceedings of the Manchester City Council, 4 March 1864, Manchester Town Hall Records, Manchester, England.

15 For the debate over sites see General Proceedings of the Manchester City Council, 4 March 1863, 23 August 1864, 29 September 1864, Manchester Town Hall Records.

16 See Cuttings File: Abel Heywood, MLHL.

17 See Cuttings File: Joseph Thompson, MLHL.

18 *Manchester Examiner and Times*, 12 September 1864.

19 See Cuttings File: Abel Heywood, MLHL.

20 See Briggs, *Victorian Cities*, p. 162.

21 Arthur Redford, *The History of Local Government in Manchester*, 3 vols. (London: Longman, 1939–40), vol. II, chap. 22. This work is indispensable for an understanding of late-Victorian politics and society in Manchester.

22 Ibid., II:410–15.

23 See "Instructions to Architects," General Proceedings of the Manchester City Council 6:133, Manchester Town Hall Records.

24 See General Proceedings of the Manchester City Council, 6 March 1867, MLHL.

25 *Builder*, 30 March, 1867.

26 T. H. Wyatt, "Explanation of Design: 'Faire Sans Dire,' " f. 7235, M3, f. 725, 13 M6A, MLHL.

27 Cuthbert Broderick, "Explanation of Design: 'Arnolfo di Lopo,' " no number, MLHL.

28 J. O. Scott, "Explanation of Design: 'Sperandum,' " f. 725, 13, M4, MLHL.

29 General Proceedings of the Manchester City Council, 1 April 1868, MLHL; *Builder*, 4 April 1868; *Manchester Guardian*, 18 March 1868, 31 March 1868.

30 Léon Faucher, *Manchester in 1844*, trans. a member of the Manchester Athaenaeum (Manchester, 1844), p. 25.

31 Waterhouse to Thompson, 13 August 1867, AL-MCRL.

32 Waterhouse to Thompson, 13 August 1867, 18 March 1868, AL-MCRL.

33 On Waterhouse's career see Stuart A. Smith, "Alfred Waterhouse, A Study in Civic Grandeur," in *Seven Victorian Architects*, ed. Jane Fawcett (London: Thames & Hudson, 1976), pp. 92–121. Also see Carroll Meeks, *The Railroad Station: An Architectural History* (New Haven: Yale University Press, 1956), p. 10.

34 *Manchester Guardian*, 8 April 1868.

35 Ibid.

36 Ibid., 2 April 1868.

37 Ibid.

38 See Ivor Webb, "The Bradford Wool Exchange: Industrial Capitalism and the Popularity of Gothic," *Victorian Studies* XX (1976):45–68. This article ignores the archival materials relating to the building of the Bradford Wool Exchange (they are located in the Bradford Central Reference Library), the Victorian literature on the wool trade, and the iconography of the building.

39 See the report of his speech in *Manchester Guardian*, 7 October 1843.

40   Quoted in *The Idea of the City in Nineteenth Century Britain*, ed. B. I. Coleman (London: Routledge & Kegan Paul, 1973), p. 160.

41   Quoted in Stewart, *The Stones of Manchester*, p. 86.

42   For the debate see *Manchester Guardian*, 7 February 1877 as well as Memorial of Isaac Gregory Urging That the Civic Buildings Be Called a Guild Hall, M79/1/27, MLHL.

43   Thompson to Waterhouse, 29 October 1876, AL-MCRL.

44   Waterhouse to Thompson, 26 October 1876, AL-MCRL.

45   Axon, *Architectural and General Description*, p. 40.

46   Ibid., p. 53.

47   Ibid., p. 48.

48   Redford, *History of Local Government in Manchester*, vol. II, chap. 22.

49   Axon, *Architectural and General Description*, p. 59.

50   For general developments see G. M. Young, *Victorian England: Portrait of an Age* (Oxford: Oxford University Press, 1976), pp. 153-87; and Sidney G. Checkland, *The Rise of Industrial Society in England, 1815–1870* (London: Longman, 1965), pp. 128–9.

51   Matthew Arnold, *Culture and Anarchy* (London, 1869), chap. 1.

52   For a scholarly statement of this traditional view see James Tait, *Medieval Manchester and the Beginnings of Lancashire* (Manchester: Victoria University Press, 1904).

53   *Manchester Guardian*, 13 September 1877.

54   On Brown see F. M. Hueffer, *Ford Madox Brown: A Record of His Life and Work* (London, 1896).

55   *British Architect*, 8 July 1876, 14 July 1877.

56   Ibid., 3 August 1877.

57   Joseph Thompson to Chairman of Town Hall Subcommittee, 8 October 1878, M79/1/10, MLHL.

58   For Brown's rationale see Brown to Thompson, 7 August 1878, AL-MCRL.

59   On nineteenth-century historical painting see Roy Strong, *And When Did You Last See Your Father? The Victorian Painter and British History* (London: Thames & Hudson, 1978). For Brown's historical research see Brown to Thompson, 7 August 1878, AL-MCRL.

60   William Axon to Abel Heywood, 23 September 1878, M79/1/9, MLHL.

61   Ibid., 23 September 1878.

62   Joseph Thompson to Chairman of Town Hall Subcommittee, 8 October 1878, M79/1/10, MLHL.

63   Brown to Waterhouse, 1 October 1878, AL-MCRL.

64   Joseph Thompson to Chairman of Town Hall Subcommittee, 8 October 1878, M79/1/10, MLHL.

65   Brown to Waterhouse, 1 October 1878, AL-MCRL.

66   Ibid.

67   Brown's description is quoted in Hueffer, *Ford Madox Brown*, pp. 371–2.

68   Ibid., p. 379.

69 Ibid., p. 386.

70 Brown to Thompson, 14 March 1878, AL-MCRL.

71 John Ruskin, "Traffic," in *The Works of John Ruskin*, ed. E. T. Cook and Alexander Wedderburn (London: Allen, 1905), 18:450–1.

72 Walter Bagehot, *The English Constitution*, Introduction by R.H.S. Crossman (Ithaca: Cornell University Press, 1966), pp 60–1.

73 Patrick Joyce, *Work, Society and Politics: The Culture of the Factory in Later Victorian England* (New Brunswick, N.J.: Rutgers University Press, 1980).

5. EPILOGUE: TRADITIONALISM AND INDUSTRIALISM

1 G. K. Clark, *The Making of Victorian England* (Cambridge, Mass.: Harvard University Press, 1962), chap. 1.

2 W. D. Rubinstein, "Wealth, Elites and the Class Structure of Modern Britain," *Past and Present* 76 (August 1977):99–126.

3 On the "British disease" see especially "What Is the British Disease?" *Times* (London), 29 April 1971; Isaac Kramnick, ed., *Is Britain Dying? Perspectives on the Current Crisis* (Ithaca: Cornell University Press, 1979).

4 Martin J. Wiener, *English Culture and the Decline of the Industrial Spirit, 1850–1980* (Cambridge: Cambridge University Press, 1981), pp. 1–25.

5 César Graña, *Fact and Symbol* (New York: Oxford University Press, 1971), p. 98.

6 Joseph Levenson, *Confucian China and Its Modern Fate*, 3 vols. (Berkeley: University of California Press, 1958–65), III:v.

7 Quoted in Ellen E. Frank, "The Domestication of Nature: Five Houses in the Lake District," in *Nature and the Victorian Imagination*, ed. U. C. Knoepflmacher and G. B. Tennyson (Berkeley: University of California Press, 1977) p. 68.

8 Quoted in George H. Ford, "Felicitous Space: The Cottage Controversy," in *Nature and the Victorian Imagination*, ed. Knoepflmacher and Tennyson, p. 47.

9 Walter Bagehot, *The English Constitution*, Introduction by R.H.S. Crossman (Ithaca: Cornell University Press, 1966), p. 250.

10 Ibid., p. 59.

11 S. N. Eisenstadt analyzes the interaction between tradition and modernity in *Tradition, Change and Modernity* (New York: Wiley, 1973), chap. 1.

Bibliographical essay

The aim of this bibliography is to provide a convenient guide to the major primary sources used in the preparation of this study and to the existing scholarly literature; it is not intended to be exhaustive.

1. THE PARADOXES OF PROGRESS

There is no comparative analysis of European medievalism in the eighteenth and nineteenth centuries. For eighteenth-century attitudes see Kenneth Clark, *The Gothic Revival: An Essay in the History of Taste* (1962); Arthur O. Lovejoy, "The First Gothic Revival and the Return to Nature," *Modern Language Notes* XLVII (1932); Reinhard Haferkorn, *Gotik und Ruine in der englischen Dichtung des achtzehnten Jahrhunderts* (1924); Paul Yvon, *Le Gothique et la Renaissance Gothique en Angleterre 1750–1880* (1931); W. D. Robson-Scott, *The Literary Background of the Gothic Revival in Germany* (1965); Georg Germann, *The Gothic Revival in Europe and Britain: Sources, Influences and Ideas* (1978); and Montague Summers, *The Gothic Quest: A History of the Gothic Novel* (1964).

Although everyone knows about the romantic infatuation with the Middle Ages, there is no good general work on the subject. There is some useful information in Gottfried Salomon, *Das Mittelalter als Ideal in der Romantik* (1922); Alice Chandler, *A Dream of Order: The Medieval Ideal in Nineteenth Century English Literature* (1971); and Janine R. Dakyns, *The Middle Ages in French Literature, 1851–1900* (1973). See especially Hugh Honour, *Romanticism* (1979).

The literature on Victorian medievalism approaches the subject through art history, literary history, and biography. The classic works on the Gothic Revival are Kenneth Clark, *The Gothic Revival: An Essay in the History of Taste*, and Charles Eastlake, *A History of the Gothic Revival* (1872). James F. White, *The Cambridge Movement: The Ecclesiologists and the Gothic Revival* (1962), is particularly useful on the interconnections between the religious and the Gothic revivals. Although Alice Chandler's *The Medieval Ideal in Nineteenth Century English Literature* does not present significant

reinterpretations of the lives and works of English literary figures, it does interrelate the visions of Scott, Cobbett, Coleridge, Carlyle, Pugin, Disraeli, Ruskin, Morris, and Adams. On Pugin see especially Phoebe Stanton, *Pugin* (1971), as well as Denis Gwynn, *Lord Shrewsbury, Pugin and the Catholic Revival* (1946), and Michael Trappes-Lomax, *Pugin: A Mediaeval Victorian* (1933). On Young England see Charles Whibley, *Lord John Manners and His Friends*, 2 vols. (1924), and Paul Smith, "The Young England Movement," Ph.D. dissertation, Columbia University, 1951. For Disraeli and Young England see Robert Blake, *Disraeli* (1966). The medieval preoccupations of the Pre-Raphaelite painter-poets can be illuminated by using the vast bibliocritical study by William E. Fredeman, *Pre-Raphaelitism: A Bibliographical Study* (1965). It is not surprising that William Morris's medievalism has attracted considerable scholarly attention. On Morris's medievalism and his debt to the ideas of Carlyle and Ruskin see E. P. Thompson, *William Morris: Romantic to Revolutionary* (1977); Margaret Grennan, *William Morris: Medievalist and Revolutionary* (1945); and R. Furneaux Jordan, *The Medieval Vision of William Morris* (1960).

Although much has been written about Victorian medievalism from the vantage point of the lives and works of artists and thinkers, it would still be very useful to have a work that analyzes the interrelationships between different spheres of art and thought.

For the popular interest in the Middle Ages *The Illustrated London News* (1842–) is invaluable. On Edward Freeman, see W.R.W. Stephens, *The Life and Letters of Edward Freeman*, 2 vols. (1895). The most valuable material on Freeman is in manuscript. See especially his correspondence with James Bryce in the Bryce Papers, Bodleian Library, Oxford; his correspondence with John Richard Green in the Freeman-Green Papers, Jesus College, Oxford; and his correspondence with W. E. Gladstone in the Gladstone Papers, the British Library. There is also some useful material in the University of Edinburgh Library and in Dr. Williams's Library, London.

2. THE VISION OF HISTORY

The basic sources on the archeological societies discussed in the text are the Yorkshire Archaeological Society, Leeds; the Bradford Historical and Antiquarian Society, Bradford; and the Sussex Archaeological Society, Lewes. These must be supplemented by their journals: *Yorkshire Archaeological and Topographical Journal* (1870–); *The Bradford Antiquary* (1888–); and *Sussex Archaeological Collections* (1848–).

This chapter is based on an exhaustive examination of Victorian guidebooks in the British Museum. Of special significance were *The Handbook for Hastings, St. Leonard's and Their Neighbourhood* (1845); *The Historical Guide to Leeds* (1858); *British Association for the Advancement of Science Guide to Sheffield* (1879); *The Exeter Guide and Itinerary* (1836); *The Handy Guide to Bradford* (1873); *Handbook to Bradford and the Neighbourhood*

(1900); *Guide to Manchester and Salford* (1878); *Ready Guide and Tourist's Handbook for Sussex* (1878); *Tourist's Picturesque Guide to Nottingham and Its Environs* (1871); *A Description of York* (1823); *A Guide to the City of York* (1838); *New Guide to the City of Exeter and Its Environs* (1824); *Hastings Past and Present* (1855); *A Visit to Sherwood Forest* (1850); *The Handbook to the City of Norwich* (1883); and Lawrence's *Illustrated Guide to Leicester* (1868).

Victorians wrote voluminously about the histories of their town, cities, and counties. The most useful general surveys are Edward Freeman and William Hunt, eds., *Historic Towns*, 11 vols. (1889–95); E. A. Freeman, *English Towns and Districts* (1883); and John Doran, *Memoirs of Our Great Towns* (1878). For a representative sampling of local histories see J. Bigland, *A Topographical and Historical Description of the County of York* (1819); J. J. Sheahan and T. Whellan, *The History of Topography of the City of York* (1855); J. Orange, *History and Antiquities of Nottingham* (1853); A. D. Bayne, *Royal Illustrated History of Eastern England*, 2 vols. (1880); J. A. Picton, *Memorials of Liverpool*, 2 vols. (1873); W. H. Wylie, *History of Nottingham* (1893); J. F. Nicholls and J. Taylor, *Bristol Past and Present*, 3 vols. (1881–2); W. J. Loftie, *A History of London* (1883); J. James, *The History and Topography of Bradford* (1841); J. Fawcett, *The Rise and Progress of the Town and Borough of Bradford* (1859); T. Baines, ed., *Yorkshire Past and Present*, 3 vols. (1878); W.E.A. Axon, *The Annals of Manchester* (1886); J. Wheeler, *Manchester, Its Political, Social and Commercial History, Ancient and Modern*, 2 vols. (1861); Mark Antony Lower, *Chronicles of Pevensey* (1846); R. L. Kirby, *Ancient Middlesbrough: Gleanings of Local History*, Middlesbrough (1900); and *Topographical and Historical Account of the City of Norwich, Its Antiquities and Modern Improvements* (1849).

For the King Alfred millenary celebrations the indispensable contemporary source is Alfred Bowker, *The Millenary of King Alfred* (1902). For Harrison's historical work see Frederic Harrison, *The Meaning of History* (1889).

For eighteenth- and nineteenth-century attitudes toward the past the following are all valuable: Stuart Piggott, *William Stukeley* (1950); Stuart Piggott, *Ruins in a Landscape* (1976); Joan Evans, *History of the Society of Antiquaries* (1956); Esther Moir, *The Discovery of Britain: The English Tourists* (1964); T. D. Kendrick, *British Antiquity* (1950); Asa Briggs, *Saxons, Normans and Victorians* (1966); John W. Burrow, "'The Village Community' and the Uses of History in Late Nineteenth Century England," in *Historical Perspectives: Studies in English Thought and Society in Honour of J. H. Plumb*, ed. Neil McKendrick (1975); Jerome Hamilton Buckley, *The Triumph of Time: A Study of the Victorian Concepts of Time, History, Progress and Decadence* (1967); G. P. Gooch, *History and Historians in the Nineteenth Century* (1959); Duncan Forbes, *The Liberal Anglican Idea of History* (1952); Olive Anderson, "The Political Uses of History in Mid-nineteenth Century England," *Past and Present* 36 (1967); Christopher Hill, "The Norman Yoke," *Puritanism and Revolution* (1958); T. W. Mason, "Nineteenth-Century Crom-

well," *Past and Present* 40 (1968); and John R. Hale, *England and the Italian Renaissance: The Growth of Interest in Its History and Art* (1954).

3. THE PRESERVATION OF THE PAST

Perhaps the most useful book on historic preservation in the nineteenth and twentieth centuries is Jane Fawcett, ed., *The Future of the Past* (1976). Aspects of restoration and preservation are examined in S. T. Madsen, *Restoration and Anti-Restoration* (1976); James F. White, *The Cambridge Movement: The Ecclesiologists and the Gothic Revival* (1962); Wayland Young, *Preservations* (1972); and Peter Ferriday, "The Church Restorers," *Architectural Review* CXXXVI (1964). For an excellent analysis of the French scene see Anthony Sutcliffe, *The Autumn of Central Paris: The Defeat of Town Planning, 1850–1970* (1970). Interesting contemporary conceptions are presented in Kevin Lynch, *What Time Is This Place?* (1972).

On the SPAB see *Annual Reports of the Society for the Protection of Ancient Buildings* (1877–). For the stories of Kirkstall Abbey, the York city churches, and countless other buildings see the Society for the Protection of Ancient Buildings Archives. Local reactions on the course of events in Leeds are best followed in the *Leeds Mercury* and on those in York in the *York Herald*. The collection on Kirkstall Abbey in the Leeds Local History Library is invaluable. Philip H. Delamotte and Joseph Cundall, *A Photographic Tour among the Abbeys of Yorkshire* (1856), has some excellent photographs of Kirkstall Abbey before it was renovated in the early 1890s. There is much useful information in W. H. St. John Hope and John Bilson, "Architectural Description of Kirkstall Abbey," *The Publications of the Thoresby Society* XVI (1907). For descriptions of the York city churches see *The Churches of York* (1843), *The Visitor's Guide to the Cathedral and City of York* (1869), and the *Illustrated Penny Guide to York* (1879).

4. THE ARCHITECTURE OF THE INDUSTRIAL CITY

The documentation of the making of the Manchester Town Hall is immense. The essential sources are the manuscripts, printed matter, and illustrations in the Manchester Town Hall Records, the Manchester Central Reference Library, and the Manchester Local History Library. Local reactions are recorded in the *Manchester Guardian* and also in *Momus, The British Architect*, and *The City Jackdaw*. For the views of the professional community see the *Builder* and the *Building News*. There is useful information on Alfred Waterhouse and Ford Madox Brown in Stuart Allen Smith, "Alfred Waterhouse," Ph.D. dissertation, London University (1970), and F. M. Hueffer, *Ford Madox Brown: A Record of His Life and Work* (1896). See also the Waterhouse Papers, Royal Institute of British Architects, London. William Axon, *An Architectural and General Description of the Town Hall, Manchester* (1878), is an invaluable contemporary report. There is, of

course, no substitute for spending time in and around the Manchester Town Hall and touring the streets of Manchester.

For the Victorian architectural background see Cecil Stewart, *The Stones of Manchester* (1956); Kenneth Clark, *The Gothic Revival: An Essay in the History of Taste* (1962); Charles Eastlake, *A History of the Gothic Revival* (1872); George Hersey, *High Victorian Gothic: A Study in Associationism* (1972); Peter Ferriday, ed., *Victorian Architecture* (1963); R. Furneaux Jordan, *Victorian Architecture* (1963); John Summerson, *Victorian Architecture: Four Studies in Evaluation* (1971); Stefan Muthesius, *The High Victorian Movement in Architecture, 1850–70* (1972); H. R. Hitchcock, *Early Victorian Architecture* (1954); M. H. Port, *Six Hundred New Churches: A Study of the Church Building Commission, 1818–1856* (1961); Mark Girouard, *The Victorian Country House* (1971); M. H. Port, ed., *The Houses of Parliament* (1976); Peter Collins, *Changing Ideals in Modern Architecture, 1750–1950* (1965); Frank Jenkins, *Architect and Patron* (1961); and Carroll Meeks, *The Railroad Station: An Architectural History* (1956). On historical painting see Roy Strong, *And When Did You Last See Your Father? The Victorian Painter and British History* (1978).

Scholars have used Manchester as a laboratory to observe the process of modernization. The best general essay is A.J.P. Taylor, "Manchester," *Essays in English History* (1976). For the Manchester of the 1840s see, above all, Asa Briggs, *Victorian Cities* (1975). Steven Marcus, *Engels, Manchester and the Working Class* (1974), is particularly good on perceptions of Manchester. Two recent contributions to the subject of Manchester history are John D. Wirth and Robert L. Jones, *Manchester and San Paolo: Problems of Rapid Urban Growth* (1978), and Maurice Spiers, *Victoria Park, Manchester: A Nineteenth Century Suburb in Its Social and Administrative Context* (1976). Although the law of diminishing returns seems to have set in concerning the study of early-Victorian Manchester, much remains to be done on the late-Victorian scene. Arthur Redford, *The History of Local Government in Manchester*, 3 vols. (1939–40), is indispensable. Dorothy Shena Simon, *A Century of City Government* (1938), is also useful. G. F. Chadwick, "The Face of the Industrial City: Two Looks at Manchester," *The Victorian City: Images and Reality*, ed. H. J. Dyos and Michael Wolff, 2 vols. (1978), vol. II, is a suggestive visual tour of Manchester in the 1840s and the 1890s. It does not discuss changing architectural styles.

Index

Adams, Henry, 19
Akroyd, Edward, 99, 100, 106
Alfred, king of England
  celebration of millenary of, 72–5
  Victorian views of, 71–2
Ancient Middlesbrough, 66
Anti–Corn Law League, 30, 68
"Anti-Scrape"; *see* Society for
    the
Protection of Ancient Buildings
antiquities
  attitudes to, 37–41, 43–5
  the sense of place and, 41
  tourism and, 39, 40, 41, 43, 44, 45
  see also Lewes, discovery of
    medieval remains at
archeological and historical
    societies
  pre-Victorian, 46
  reasons for similarities in
    Yorkshire and Sussex, 57–8
  Victorian proliferation of, 46–9
  see also Bradford Historical and
    Antiquarian Society; Sussex
    Archaeological Society;
    Yorkshire Archaeological and
    Topographical Society
Arnold, Matthew, 69, 109, 143, 144,
    160, 162
  Culture and Anarchy, 143,
    160
Arnold, Thomas, 1
Artisan and Labourers' Dwelling
    Act, 146
Ashbee, C. R., 89

Axon, William
  on the architecture of the
    Manchester New Town Hall,
    136–7
  on the proposed subjects for the
    Manchester New Town Hall
    murals, 164–5, 166

Bagehot, Walter
  on deference and tradition, 29,
    174–5, 181
  The English Constitution, 174
Barrow-in-Furness Town Hall, 140
Barry, Sir Charles, 6
Belcher, J. and J., 8
Bennett, B. E., 101, 102
Bennett, S. H., 123
Birmingham, 80, 108, 140, 155, 159
Birmingham and Midland Institute,
    48, 72
Birmingham Daily Post
  on Kirkstall Abbey, 103, 106–7
Blaauw, W. H., 35, 36, 50, 51, 52
Bodley, George Frederick, 132
Bowker, Alfred
  and millenary of King Alfred, 72,
    73, 74
Bradford, 41, 67, 173–4
Bradford Historical and Antiquarian
    Society, 48, 50
  aims of, 52
  Bradford Antiquary, 33, 56, 65
  historical interests of, 55–6
  membership of, 51
Bradford Town Hall, 140

Index